THE GARDEN OF:

SWEET

PEA

SCHOOL

SWEET PE

Marryn Mathis

Photographs by Christine Chitnis

Growing
&
Arranging
the
Garden's
Most
Romantic
Blooms

SCHOOL

CHRONICLE BOOKS
San Francisco

Library of Congress Cataloging-in-Publication Data

Names: Mathis, Marryn, author. | Chitnis, Christine, photographer.
Title: Sweet pea school : growing and arranging the garden's most romantic blooms / Marryn Mathis ; photographs by Christine Chitnis
Description: San Francisco, California : Chronicle Books, 2025
Identifiers: LCCN 2024029708 | ISBN 9781797228426 (hardcover)
Subjects: LCSH: Sweet peas. | Flower gardening.
Classification: LCC SB413.S9 M38 2025 | DDC 633.3/6--dc23/eng/20240711
LC record available at https://lccn.loc.gov/2024029708

Manufactured in China.

Design by Lizzie Vaughan.
Typesetting by Wynne Au-Yeung.

10 9 8 7 6 5 4 3 2 1

Chronicle books and gifts are available at special quantity discounts to corporations, professional associations, literacy programs, and other organizations. For details and discount information, please contact our premiums department at corporatesales@chroniclebooks.com or at 1-800-759-0190.

Chronicle Books LLC
680 Second Street
San Francisco, California 94107
www.chroniclebooks.com

THE MAGIC OF SWEET PEAS

My sweet pea patch, with its climbing tendrils reaching skyward and plentiful blooms, is tucked between our old wooden barn and an ancient apple orchard. It is my sanctuary, my playground, and my classroom. When the warm days of summer finally arrive and the colors of the evening sky are echoed in the rows of lush sweet peas, there is no place that I'd rather be. As I walk through the towering vines, I'm surrounded by thousands of fragrant blooms, and it feels as though I'm swimming in a sea of flowers. Among these nostalgic blooms, I feel an excitement to learn, a curiosity to try new things, an acceptance when I fail, and a deep satisfaction when my hard work pays off. In a way, the plants and I nurture and take care of each other. I tend to them, and in turn, they feed my soul.

Sweet peas were one of my grandma's favorite flowers. I remember as a little girl sitting on my grandma's lap listening as she told me about the scent of sweet peas and the beauty of their blooms. Sadly, she couldn't grow sweet peas in her own garden because of a deer problem, and so it was her stories that brought them to life for me. Her love of these flowers also echoed in the little touches of sweet peas in her embroidery and on her handkerchiefs. These memories from my childhood have stayed with me, and I've always shared my grandma's appreciation for

this gentle bloom, but it wasn't until I grew them for myself that my full-blown love affair began. Little did I know that the moment I put that first seed in the soil was the start of something life changing. As I stood for the first time in front of those incredible vines laden with sugary-sweet blooms, I was completely smitten by the way their delicate petals danced in the breeze, their heavy sweet fragrance filled the air, and their curly tendrils exuded romance. In that moment, it was as if all the rest of the world stood still, and what I was meant to do with my life became clear. I was meant to grow sweet peas.

FALLING IN LOVE WITH SWEET PEAS: MY JOURNEY

My journey with flowers didn't start until later in life. After working in IT for over twenty years, I had a feeling that there was another chapter to my life, just waiting to be written. I didn't know what my calling was yet, but I knew sitting in a cubicle behind a desk wasn't it. After some soul-searching, my husband and I made some tough decisions, and I walked away from corporate America. It was terrifying to leave behind a solid paycheck and health care benefits, but at the same time exhilarating to think of all the possibilities that lay ahead.

I like to say the flowers found me, because looking back, it feels as though flower farming just came into my life out of nowhere. I had grown a garden in our suburban backyard, but the idea of farming was completely foreign to me. At the time, flower farming was just becoming more mainstream. Photos of lush backyard farms were starting to appear in magazines and online. From the moment I first saw images of flowering rows and beautifully wrapped bouquets, I knew that this was my next calling. It was almost as though looking at those photos planted a seed in my soul that I needed to tend and nurture so that I myself could grow. So I invested in an online course and ordered a stack of gardening books, and our search for a farm began. It wasn't picture-perfect, and it certainly wasn't easy, but after a few twists and turns in our journey—one such twist involved our family of five living in a 28-foot-long travel trailer for two years—we found our forever farm.

Sweet peas have had my heart from the very start. As I entered into my inaugural year of flower farming, the earliest seeds to kick off the spring planting were those of the sweet pea. I remember that as I tucked them nervously into the dirt, I thought about my grandma and her love of this flower.

A few weeks later, the first shoots started to emerge. They looked like tiny snake heads as they reached for the light. They were my first plant babies, and I watched over them like a mother hen.

While those tiny sprouts were growing in the greenhouse, the field too was coming to life. We laid down rows of landscape fabric and brought in fresh compost, set up supports, and hung netting for the vines to climb on. We were ready. I tucked the sweet peas from the greenhouse into the field, and with that, our first plants were officially in the ground. I watched and waited for what seemed like an eternity before I saw even the slightest change. Then one day, little green stubs of new growth began to emerge, and seemingly overnight, the vines shot up like rockets. It wasn't long before I was looking at our first real blooms.

I put our row of sweet peas at the edge of our field under the shade of some trees. They got full sun until the early afternoon hours, then enjoyed shade and shelter from the afternoon heat. I wish I could say I planned it that way, but honestly, it was beginner's luck. The plants loved it, and the vines exploded into bloom. Their frilly petals, the sweet fragrance paired with their delicate yet tough nature: I loved everything about them.

From those first few rows, my sweet pea patch has now grown to over twenty thousand plants, and my love for these blooms continues to grow, season after season.

My goal is not just to teach you all of my tips and tricks so that you too can grow amazing sweet peas in your own garden, but also to nurture and support the gardener and grower within you. I want you to be successful with sweet peas, and in some cases this might mean trying something new or doing things differently than you have in the past. Are you a confirmed soaker of your seeds prior to sowing them? Maybe you've never fall-sown your sweet peas or you've given your seedlings too much heat so they bolted quickly, becoming leggy and floppy, and never fully recovered. Well, I am here to help! My hope is that as you turn the pages ahead, you not only are inspired and feel my love and passion for these incredible flowers, but also know I'm right here beside you, cheering you on every step of the way.

You get what you give with sweet peas; if you give them the support and care they need, I promise you will be rewarded with healthy, towering vines and loads of stunning stems.

WHY SWEET PEAS DESERVE SPACE IN YOUR GARDEN

This probably won't come as a surprise, but I believe no garden is complete without a few rows of sweet peas tucked in there. Grown in gardens around the world for hundreds of years, sweet peas are rich in history, with a lineage that has been passed down through generations of devoted gardeners. While walking through my garden, I like to imagine those who came before me, who were equally devoted to this beautiful bloom. Where did they source their seeds? What colors brought them the most joy? What was the world like at that time? What did these flowers mean to them?

Often, when I meet a gardener who hasn't yet experienced the unrivaled beauty and fragrance of sweet peas, they tell me they haven't added them to their garden lineup because (1) they are too much work, and (2) they take up too much space. In reality, sweet peas don't have to be a lot of work (see "Easy to Grow" on page 16). And unlike many other flower types, sweet peas actually take up very little space (see "Require Little Space" on page 17). They don't have to be grown in long rows like we do here at the farm. I suggest you think outside the box: Perhaps you have a fence or an arbor that they can climb on, or a pot on your deck with some bamboo poles or an obelisk.

But to elaborate, here are my top reasons why you should give sweet peas a shot in your garden.

BEAUTIFUL Sweet peas are a true standout in the garden: With their heads held high, they exude sophistication and elegance, yet they are incredibly simple and approachable. Whether it's a single bloom in a bud vase, a handful in a Mason jar, or a few stems used as an accent in a bridal bouquet, sweet peas offer beautiful versatility as cut flowers.

FRAGRANT There are few things more intoxicating than burying your nose in a bouquet of freshly cut sweet peas. A single inhale can transport you to another place and time. I've witnessed people that get lost in their aroma and instantly return to memories of their grandma's garden. In the summer, a garden with sweet peas beckons you with its fragrance wafting in the warm breeze. Here on the farm, I can smell our sweet pea patch as soon as I come outside in the morning, and visitors often say they can smell them even before they arrive on our property. Like the return of an old friend, it's a scent I look forward to every year. What's even better? There is a range of different scents depending on the variety! Sweet peas are assigned a rating on the scent scale ranging from 1 (very little scent) to 6 (extremely fragrant). Their fragrance can also be affected by temperatures, rain, and flower maturity. So if you're someone who grows flowers based on their fragrance, then look no further: The sweet pea is for you.

EASY TO GROW Contrary to popular belief, sweet peas are one of the easiest flowers to grow. They have an undeserved reputation for being fragile, delicate blooms that demand care and maintenance. That couldn't be further from the truth. These guys are tough! They can endure frost like nobody's business, and the cooler conditions are, the more they thrive. They can be as simple or as high maintenance as you want. If you are growing sweet peas just for your garden, I suggest planting, then leaving them mostly alone to do their thing. If you're growing them for cut flowers, I recommend keeping them corralled and tied to their trellis to encourage longer stems (more on this in chapter 4). But bottom line: Growing sweet peas isn't rocket science.

A GREAT CUT FLOWER Sweet peas are one of the most popular flowers for bouquets and arrangements for several key reasons. Their versatility is unparalleled. Their long stems make them the ideal cut flower. They come in a rainbow of stunning colors. And their scents range on a scale from the slightest hint of sugar to candied citrus and perfumes so heady they can fill a room.

POLLINATOR FRIENDLY We gardeners are not alone in our love of sweet peas; they are a favorite among pollinators as well, drawn irresistibly to the colorful blooms rich in nectar and pollen. Our sweet pea patch here on the farm is constantly buzzing with bees, butterflies, and other flying insects, as well as hummingbirds and other birds who feed on the insect bounty. If your goal is to create a more biodiverse garden, a few rows of sweet peas will take you far.

LONG GROWING SEASON Sweet peas are the gift that keeps on giving: The more you cut them, the more they grow. If you keep up with harvesting and give them the right conditions, you'll enjoy blooms from June to September.

REQUIRE LITTLE SPACE Unlike with other cut flowers, the trick with sweet pea planning is to think vertically, not horizontally. Sweet pea vines grow tall and narrow, so they don't take up much space. As long as you can provide them with some support, the sky's the limit. I recommend using whatever you have available to you. Whether it's an existing fence, an arbor, or a panel of hog wire fencing along the side of your house, when it comes to sweet peas, aim high.

EASY SEED SAVING You can collect seed right from your existing sweet pea plants for next year's stock, and the good news is that their seeds are some of the easiest to save. They are what we in the seed world call *selfers*, which means they self-pollinate, and the seed that you collect will grow to be the exact same variety as its parent plant. For example, the seed that comes from 'Blue Shift' will produce more 'Blue Shift' plants next year. If you are growing more than one variety and want to grow a mix, throw all of those brown dried pods into a brown paper bag, and just like that, you've got your own special combination of sweet pea varieties for next year!

Come along with me as I take you on a journey through my sweet pea patch. Feel the wonder of these romantic blooms while I teach you all of my tips and tricks for growing gorgeous sweet peas right in your own garden. Surround yourself with their delicate beauty and towering vines; drink in their intoxicating fragrance. See why sweet peas have captivated flower lovers for hundreds of years, and learn how to take your bouquets and arrangements from ordinary to extraordinary by adding just a few sweet pea stems. My love for sweet peas runs deep, and my hope with this book is that with every turn of the page you too can feel their magic.

I.

THE
HISTORY OF
SWEET PEAS

Sweet peas have long been considered quintessentially English flowers of the Victorian era. For many people, sweet peas call to mind abundant gardens tended by women in petticoat dresses who sipped their afternoon tea surrounded by fragrant beauty. So it may surprise you to learn that sweet peas originated in the hills of Sicily, the largest island region of Italy. In the late 1600s, a Sicilian monk and botanist named Francesco Cupani discovered wild sweet peas on a hillside. Those early wildflowers were untamed, bright, small, and quite short, much different from the sweet peas we know and love today.

My sweet pea–loving heart can't help but wonder what that moment must've been like for Cupani as he came upon this discovery. What I wouldn't give to be able to sit down with him and hear what went through his mind when he laid eyes on them for the very first time! Was he completely captivated by them? Did he stare at them in wonder? Did he know that these tiny flowers would change the gardening landscape over the course of hundreds of years and become what they are today? We will never know, but one thing is sure: Those magical flowers seem to have cast their spell on him. Cupani must've known that he was onto something very special in 1695, as he collected seeds from those first wild sweet peas and shared them with plant collectors and various gardens throughout England.

BREEDING

After their initial discovery in 1695, sweet peas remained relatively unchanged for the next two hundred years, with only a few new varieties emerging, as mutations and *sports* (see Glossary, page 237) were collected and grown out. It wasn't until the late 1800s that Henry Eckford's breeding efforts changed the future of sweet peas forever.

Since then the face of sweet peas has changed dramatically. What started out as a small, simple, brightly colored wildflower has been transformed into a cherished staple in today's gardens, with regal blooms fit for a queen. No longer limited as in the days of old, the sweet pea rainbow is now a kaleidoscope of color with a vast array to choose from. Today, flowers range from the purest of whites to the blackest purple, with an extensive menu of sizes and heights and growing habits, from towering Spencers, to dwarf varieties that are perfect for pots, to perennials that come back year after year. There is definitely a sweet pea for every garden.

For those wanting to experience those small simple wildflowers, just as Cupani did all those years ago, don't worry! Those wild sweet peas have not only stood the test of time but also sprouted a gorgeous family tree that has since grown and blossomed into something that I doubt even Cupani could've ever envisioned. Beyond those treasured first few blooms on the Sicilian hillside, over 150 species have been discovered and included in the *Lathyrus* sweet pea *genus* (see Glossary, page 237). The most common is *Lathyrus odoratus,* which is what most gardeners associate with sweet peas due to their fragrance and nostalgic blooms. But the genus also includes the perennial *Lathyrus latifolius,* the unscented wild sweet peas.

All of the new varieties that we now know and have come to treasure are thanks to not only an endless love of sweet peas but also the hard work and determination of so many who have come before us. Their tireless work and dedication is rooted deep in history, and their love and passion for these incredible flowers can be felt in every bloom.

POPULAR BREEDERS

HENRY ECKFORD

In the late 1800s, Scottish horticulturist Henry Eckford began his life's work with sweet peas. Eckford had previously bred dahlias and various other plants, but he is best known as "father of the sweet pea" for his hybridization and breeding work with these flowers. In 1888, Eckford moved to Wem in Shropshire, England; in his later years there, his work resulted in over two hundred new sweet pea varieties, with greatly improved bloom size, increased flower production, and improved plant health. Thanks to Eckford, Wem is still known as "where the sweet peas grow." Every year, the town hosts the Wem Sweet Pea Show, which devotes an entire class to pre-1910 varieties in homage to Henry Eckford and his sweet peas.

ROGER PARSONS

A legend in the sweet pea world, British horticulturist Roger Parsons fell in love with these flowers at an early age. As a small child in his family's garden, he started growing sweet peas and saving his own seed. He remembers shopping at Woolworth's with his mother and asking for six varieties of Spencer sweet peas instead of candy. Parsons tended those early plants and was surprised the following season when they self-seeded. He observed that half of the varieties reverted back to their earlier genetic forms—his first lesson in the phenomenon of *genetic drift* in plant populations (see Glossary, page 237). Parsons started growing sweet peas seriously in 1984 and has been growing them ever since—though he didn't start breeding sweet peas until the early 1990s, when he began making his first *crosses* (new varieties created by transferring the pollen from one plant to another).

Parsons's first named sweet pea, 'Strawberry Ice', was introduced in 1997 by the venerable E. W. King & Co (a breeder and seed supplier founded in 1888). The following year, Parsons started his own personal seed bank, now recognized as the National Collection of Sweet Peas, with over 1,300 different sweet pea *cultivars* (see Glossary, page 237). As of this writing, Parsons is the president of the National Sweet Pea Society and to date has bred over a hundred named varieties. Over the years, he has won numerous prestigious awards for his sweet peas, including the Henry Eckford Memorial Medal, the highest honor in the sweet pea world.

As an avid lover and grower of sweet peas, I was privileged to visit with Roger Parsons at his farm in Chichester while on a trip to England in 2022. When I asked him his favorite variety, he said it would have to be 'Alison Louise', a variety he bred and named after his lovely wife.

THE NATIONAL COLLECTION

When I started growing sweet peas, it didn't take very long before the obsession took hold. I couldn't get my hands on enough of them. I was completely captivated by their beauty and in awe of how each variety is so similar to others yet so distinctive. Every variety I saw, I wanted to grow. Every color, every size, every type.

In my quest to increase my own collection, I discovered the National Collection. The holy grail of sweet peas, it is actually the personal collection of Roger Parsons, intended to collect all sweet pea cultivars from around the world to preserve and protect them for future generations. The collection now contains all known sweet pea cultivars to date, in quantities ranging from just a few seeds to a bit more stock.

DR. KEITH HAMMETT

Dr. Keith Hammett, a world-renowned plant breeder based in New Zealand, is best known for his work with sweet peas and dahlias.

Dr. Hammett became interested in sweet peas as a young teenager when he began exhibiting his uncle's sweet peas in local and national shows in England. He has been growing and breeding sweet peas since 1958. He has been recognized by the Royal Horticultural Society, which awarded him the coveted Veitch Memorial Medal for his breeding work. Dr. Hammett has bred over sixty named varieties and is most famous for his color-shifting varieties such as 'Future Shock', 'Turquoise Lagoon', 'Blue Vein', and one of my personal favorites, 'Blue Shift'. It can take seven to ten years of breeding a new variety before it becomes available to the general public. Dr. Hammett is always looking to create something that does not already exist, like *reverse bicolored* varieties (which reverse the classic coloring of the different flower parts) or those that morph in color as they age. His current work involves a major project focused on scent, strengthening the intensity of aroma and identifying individual selections by the aroma notes they display.

PHIL JOHNSON

A rising star in the world of sweet pea breeding, Phil Johnson first fell in love with sweet peas as a young boy in Britain in 1970. Keen gardeners in his family fostered his early interest, and by the late 1990s he was a seasoned exhibitor at the National Sweet Pea Society shows. In 1998, Phil was eager to further his expertise and began breeding sweet peas, although his renowned breeding program didn't start in earnest until 2014. Phil's breeding program is now one of the largest in the world and has produced dozens of exciting new colors and varieties. A few of Phil's introductions so far include 'Suffolk Punch Miggie', 'Chrissie', 'Our Heroes', 'Platinum Jubilee', 'Magenta Moments', 'Raspberry Sundae', 'Minette Marrin', and 'Serenity Remembered'. Phil's favorite types of sweet peas are the Modern Grandifloras and Semi-Grandifloras, as they are the best for the home gardener, for ease of growing, the highest quantity of blooms, and the strongest scent.

II.

TYPES OF
SWEET PEAS

With over 150 different species of sweet peas, there literally is a sweet pea for everyone and every garden, no matter your preference or space. If I were to cover all of them, this book would be quite lengthy and more of a sweet pea encyclopedia. That's not my intention (although a sweet pea encyclopedia would be a great addition to any floral library!). Instead, I've kept it to five types of sweet peas that are readily available, that you may already be familiar with, and that you will most definitely want to grow in your own garden.

Key considerations for growing sweet peas include not only your climate and USDA growing zone, but also the types of sweet pea that will best fit your circumstances. These factors can make all the difference between the success or failure of your sweet peas. Many gardeners don't know that a sweet pea's bloom cycle is triggered by the amount of daylight hours they receive. This means the practice of *succession planting* won't work for sweet peas (see Glossary, page 237). If you are growing in a challenging setting, knowing this piece of information, paired with what type of sweet peas will be best for you, can actually give you an advantage over Mother Nature.

Each of these types is quite exquisite in its own way, and even though they are all from the *Lathyrus* genus, each offers distinct qualities and characteristics, with varying heights and stem length, bloom size, hours required to induce the bloom cycle, and scents. Let me show you why the versatility of these beauties is unmatched.

SPENCERS

When it comes to sweet peas, I get a wide range of questions, from best growing practices to how to diagnose specific issues, but the most common is: *What is your favorite sweet pea?* Though it may sound cliché, I really do love them all, but I tend to gravitate toward the Spencer varieties.

If you've grown sweet peas before, I'm willing to bet that you've grown some Spencer varieties, as they're the most common type of sweet pea. Spencers have captivated gardeners and growers for over a century, and it's easy to see why. Among most flowers, there always seems to be a "queen" that stands out above the rest. Just as 'Cafe au Lait' is the current reigning queen of the dahlias, and 'La Belle Epoque' the queen of the tulips, the Spencer varieties reign supreme in the sweet pea world.

Spencer sweet peas were first introduced in 1901 with the first named variety, 'Countess Spencer'. Since then, all varieties with this form type—featuring long, strong stems and large ruffled petals, with four to six blooms per stem—have been classified as Spencer varieties. Spencer sweet peas make up a large majority of the varieties we see grown on today's flower farms and in backyard gardens. These qualities make them ideal for cut flower growers and designers. Spencers also come in a wide array of colors, from solids and flakes (see page 229) to bicolors and some varieties that even seem to defy classification, as they literally shift and change color as they grow. (That's right, 'King's Ransom' and 'Blue Shift', I'm looking at you.)

With the exception of yellow (a true yellow sweet pea has eluded breeders to this day, due the genetic complexity involved), Spencers come
in not only almost every color of the rainbow but also a wide range of
fragrances. Some varieties drip with sweet pea perfume, others have
just the slightest hint of fragrance, and still others have no fragrance at
all. There is as much variability in the intensity of fragrance of Spencer
sweet peas as there is variability in color.

If color, bloom size, stem length, and fragrance aren't enough to con-
vince you to try some Spencer varieties in your garden, then let's talk
about growth habits. Spencer sweet pea vines are usually the tallest
and some of the most vigorous plants here on our farm. Their towering
vines create living walls in my sweet pea patch; when given the right
support and growing conditions, they can reach 8 to 10 feet (2.4 to
3 m) in height.

Spencers require twelve hours of sunlight a day to induce the bloom
cycle. For many gardeners this isn't really an issue, but if you live in a
climate where warm temperatures (above 80°F) arrive early in the season, keep in mind that the extra hours of sunlight your blooms require
might cut your season extremely short or mean you won't see many
blooms at all. Now, I'm not saying that those of you who live in warm
climates can't fall-sow your sweet peas and see flowers before the heat
arrives in the late spring, but you might consider growing a different
type of sweet pea that doesn't require as many hours of sunlight per day.

OLD-FASHIONED

This category of blooms includes any variety with smaller flowers that dates back to pre-1914, before the larger and bolder Spencer varieties took over the sweet pea map. These old-fashioned varieties have stood the test of time, gracing gardens for over a hundred years with their dainty little blooms.

Still readily available from seed companies worldwide, old-fashioned sweet peas are recognized by their plain flowers and shorter stems. These antique heirloom varieties require twelve hours to induce the bloom cycle. What they lack in frill and stem length, they make up for in scent: These are some of the most intensely fragrant sweet peas in the *Lathyrus* genus. These single-vined plants bloom in a variety of colors and patterns, and their floral abundance is truly remarkable. Their vines, although reaching only 5 to 6 feet (1.5 to 1.8 m) tall, explode with sweet-smelling blooms.

Although I grow several old-fashioned varieties here on the farm for seed, these short-stemmed varieties don't make the best cut flowers. So unless you're considering using them in a small posy or Mason jar arrangement, these little gems are best for adding some sweet pea color and fragrance to your garden. They are perfect for planting along an existing fence line or an arbor, adding loads of charm and character to any garden space.

GRANDIFLORAS AND MODERN GRANDIFLORAS

Similar to the old-fashioned varieties, the grandifloras maintain many of their characteristics. These little darlings of the garden are still being bred today. Their small, delicate flowers and short stems are not ideal as primary flowers in arrangements, but their curly tendrils and foliage add whimsy and elegance. Grandifloras and the more current Modern Grandiflora varieties also require twelve hours of sunlight to induce the bloom cycle and produce vines laden with blooms. Their fragrance is some of the most intense that you will ever smell.

Grandifloras and Modern Grandifloras reach 5 to 6 feet (1.5 to 1.8 m) tall. With a limited color range, they often get less attention than their taller, larger, more colorful Spencer cousins. They don't get the credit that they deserve in the sweet pea world, but these tried-and-true varieties are just as charming and pretty as can be. In my opinion, they are a must-grow for any garden, whether you're a flower farmer needing to fill florists' orders for those coveted sweet pea tendrils or a backyard gardener looking for back-of-the-border beauty in your outdoor space.

SEMI-GRANDIFLORAS

Semi-Grandifloras are relatively new arrivals on the sweet pea stage.
The first variety, 'Albutt Blue', was introduced by Eagle, the renowned
Staffordshire producer, in 1999. Bred by Harvey Albutt, this new variety
combined the best of both the old-fashioned and Spencer varieties in
one incredible little flower: a beautiful white bloom edged in the most
perfect shade of purple with the highest fragrance rating.

Semi-Grandifloras blend desirable attributes of the Spencers and the
old-fashioned or grandiflora types. Their flowers have slight ruffles and
are just a touch larger than the dainty old-fashioned and grandiflora
varieties. Their stem length is longer, making these beauties great candi-
dates for cut flower growers, flower farmers, and designers.

They are highly scented, with usually four to six flowers per stem.
They come in a limited range of colors but are readily available from
seed companies and garden stores worldwide. The height of Semi-
Grandiflora plants is also vastly improved, with vines reaching over
8 feet (2.4 m) tall. These varieties require ten to twelve hours of sunlight per day to induce the bloom cycle, so if you live in a more challenging climate these might be a good option for you.

EARLY MULTIFLORAS

Growing sweet peas can be a challenge in some climates, but certain varieties, like the Early Multifloras and other winter-flowering varieties, can help make it easier. The great thing about Early Multiflora varieties that sets them apart from the rest is that they require only ten to eleven hours of sunlight a day to induce the bloom cycle. So these varieties are perfect not only for anyone trying to get blooms earlier in the year but also for those living in an area that gets warm early in the season.

Early Multiflora varieties are known for their long stems; in some cases, they are even longer than those of Spencer varieties. They have a delicious scent and large, frilly-petaled blooms, with an average of four to six flowers per stem. Early Multifloras are usually grouped in a series—'Winter Sunshine', 'Winter Elegance', 'Mammoth', 'Solstice', 'Spring Sunshine', and 'Winter Sunshine', to name a few—and within these series there are different colors. For example, the Winter Sunshine series includes:

- 'Winter Sunshine White'
- 'Winter Sunshine Cream'
- 'Winter Sunshine Lavender'
- 'Winter Sunshine Opal'
- 'Winter Sunshine Pink'
- 'Winter Sunshine Light Blue'
- 'Winter Sunshine Mid Blue'
- 'Winter Sunshine Navy'
- 'Winter Sunshine Mauve'
- 'Winter Sunshine Scarlet'
- 'Winter Sunshine Rose'

While the color range of Early Multifloras isn't quite as vast as that offered by the Spencer varieties, they more than make up for it with their early blooms. These varieties are also more disease resistant, grow beautifully throughout the winter, and are great seed producers as well.

Every year I find myself adding more and more early-flowering varieties to our sweet pea patch. Their early blooms are always a welcome sight after the gray days of winter.

III.

UNDERSTANDING SWEET PEAS

While sweet peas can be very easy to grow—just as Grandma did so effortlessly in her garden all those years ago—for those of you who have never grown them or have struggled with them in the past, there are a few key practices that can make all the difference in your sweet pea success. So before we think about planting sweet peas, I think it's important to understand a little bit more about them. (Of course, there is the emotional side—sweet peas pack such a nostalgic punch for so many of us. But a solid understanding of the practical side will help you grow the sweet peas of your dreams, with fragrance that will transport you right back to childhood summers and other long-forgotten memories.)

While I'm here partly to sell you on the magic of sweet peas, and I believe they are a must-grow in the garden when possible, it's also part of my mission with this book to be straightforward and honest about managing expectations. Those tall green walls and 2-foot-long stems don't just happen overnight. You don't need to fuss over them like a mother hen with her chicks, but you do need to follow standard practices and give them regular attention and care.

KEY ELEMENTS FOR SWEET PEAS

There are several key elements to consider when it comes to growing sweet peas. These gardening fundamentals may seem basic and feel like a no-brainer to the seasoned gardener or grower, but they're worth revisiting, as they will make all the difference in whether your sweet peas thrive or just survive.

CLIMATE Sweet peas will always have a place in my garden, but, as heartbreaking as this is for me to say, they are not a fit for everyone or every garden. Although sweet peas are versatile and come in a wide range of varieties and types, their success will depend on where you live. It's important to take your climate and USDA zone into account when deciding whether to plant sweet peas in your outdoor space.

Sweet peas like it cool; if temperatures get too warm, the plants will start to shut down, meaning they will stop blooming and either go to seed or fail to thrive. Ideally, you should keep them at or below 80°F (26.6°C). So if you live in a tropical climate that hovers around 80°F (26.6°C) for most of the year, like Hawaii or the Bahamas, I probably wouldn't recommend sweet peas for you. If you live in a warm climate that also gets some cool temperatures during the winter months, as in the southern United States, don't y'all give up hope. I will teach you some tricks to beat Mother Nature at her own game before the relentless heat of summer sets in.

Again, your climate and USDA zone will dictate what types of sweet pea you should grow, when to plant your seeds, and how to be successful growing them. Depending on where you live, you might need to grow your sweet peas a little bit differently from the practices of your flower friends in other regions. USDA growing zones have been fine-tuned, with an "a" cooler half and a "b" warmer half. For example, if you are in zone 8a or above, you need to plant earlier than those who live in zones 7 and under. Some of you might have some flexibility and the luxury of being able to plant several times a year; others have a smaller window of time in which to start seeds before it's too late.

LOCATION You know the old saying that timing is everything? Well, when it comes to sweet peas, *location* is everything. Here's my number one piece of advice for growing sweet peas: Before you even get started, before you buy that first seed packet or start getting distracted by the sweet pea rainbow, and definitely before you get those seeds into the dirt, take a moment and think about where in your garden you are going to plant them.

Here on the farm, our sweet pea patch is tucked in between two treasured landmarks, our old barn and our heirloom apple orchard. There the plants are sheltered from both scorching sun and wind.

The first year I grew sweet peas, I planted them on the far edge of my field in an area where they got full sun until the early afternoon, when they were given shade and a reprieve from the heat. Unknowingly I'd given them an optimal location, and in turn they rewarded me handsomely: I was still harvesting blooms well into October.

When choosing a location, consider your afternoon temperatures. Most sweet peas require full sun, but if your summer afternoons regularly get very hot—that is, above 80°F (26.6°C)—then I recommend planting your sweet peas in a spot with full morning sun and afternoon shade. Now, if you only have a location in full sun all day, that doesn't mean you can't or shouldn't grow sweet peas, but if you can find that sweet spot, they will thank you for it.

When choosing the best location, consider too how sweet peas grow. Unlike most other cut flowers, sweet peas like to climb, so with proper support they don't take up a lot of space in width. You will be absolutely amazed at how many flowers you can get from just a few plants. Even if you have a very small space, you can most likely accommodate a little group of sweet peas and enjoy lots of blooms come harvest. Though trellises and arbors are obvious choices, I've seen some very creative ideas from gardeners and growers who have thought outside the box. I've seen vines wrapped around tree trunks and climbing up light poles; dwarf varieties engulfing mailboxes and trailing over deck railings. For me, there is something so romantic and whimsical about leaving sweet peas to their own devices, seeing what they do and how wild they can be.

It is important to note that sweet peas are poisonous, so if you have little ones, please resist the temptation to plant your sweet peas alongside your garden peas, as it can be hard to tell the difference.

COMPOST Sweet peas are very heavy feeders. It takes a good support system underground for such vigorous growers; this means they need nice rich soil to provide nourishment all season long. In my sweet pea patch, this nourishment comes in the form of organic compost. Sweet peas love organic material, and the more compost or organic matter you can work into your soil, the better. In fact, compost is such a key element in my sweet pea patch that I add it several different times throughout the growing season—before planting, during planting, and again while the plants are getting established.

Keeping your plants happy and fed throughout the season promotes more vigorous growth, reduces stress, and helps them be able to fight off pests and disease.

WATER Sweet peas are not only hungry, they're also thirsty! How much water do they need each day? It depends on a multitude of factors, predominantly your soil type. Do you have clay soil that retains quite a bit of moisture, or sandy, loamy soil that water just goes through like a sieve? If the former, you might need to water only every other day; if the latter, every day should do the trick.

The weather, of course, is a key factor. Has there been rain in recent days? Are the temps high or mild? When it's hot, sweet peas like their roots kept as cool as possible, and this means giving them plenty of water.

Sweet peas are really good at telling you what they need; you just need to know what signs to look for. Are the leaves turning a bit yellow? You might be giving them too much water. Don't be afraid to get your hands dirty; dig a bit to see how far down the soil feels moist. You can also use a soil moisture meter to gauge what is going on beneath the surface.

TYPE The last major consideration is the type of sweet peas best suited for your area and your goals. Are you looking for early blooms or trying to beat the heat? Early Multifloras will be your key to success. Are you growing them for cut flowers and looking for good stem length, color, and fragrance? Then I recommend the Spencer, Semi-Grandiflora, or Early Multiflora varieties. Review the different types of sweet peas in chapter 2 to figure out what's best for you.

As you can see, there are many things to consider before you dig in and start getting your hands dirty, but taking the time now to understand these key factors is crucial to creating a solid foundation that will make a huge difference later on.

GARDEN SWEET PEAS OR CUT FLOWERS

Whether you're a gardener wanting to take your backyard garden from ordinary to extraordinary or a flower farmer looking to take your bouquets and arrangements to the next level, adding some sweet peas is just the ticket. But there is quite a big difference between growing sweet peas specifically for cut flowers and growing them for their beauty in your garden, so it's important to be clear on your goals before planting.

GARDEN SWEET PEAS Sweet peas have been gracing gardens for centuries with their elegant, romantic blooms. No matter how formal or informal their surroundings, whether they are in a backyard garden, display garden, or at a royal palace, sweet peas create an incredible backdrop, adding texture and whimsy. These charming chameleons can adapt to fill whatever role is asked of them. They have enough strength and vigor to play the lead, or they can be more subdued and reserved in a supporting role.

For the backyard gardener, there's nothing like watching the magic of sweet peas as they twist, turn, and flutter in the breeze. Left to their own devices, sweet peas can easily turn into what the budding flower farmer in me once thought was a wild, twisted, and tangled mess. It wasn't until I had a few years of growing under my belt that I discovered that the real magic with sweet peas is when they are in their natural state— that is when you really feel their wonder.

Growing great sweet peas in the backyard garden is surprisingly simple. As long as you give them enough support to climb and grow, they are extremely low-maintenance. If long, straight stems are not your top priority, you need only to follow the basic planting principles (see chapter 4)—some sun, water, and a little love—and you'll be seeing your first flowers in no time.

PREFERRED TYPES AND VARIETIES
FOR GARDEN SWEET PEAS

The sky is the limit for those of you just wanting to add some beauty, color, and fragrance to your garden. If stem length isn't an issue for you, here are some of my tried-and-true favorites that would make great additions to any backyard garden:

- 'Turquoise Lagoon'
- 'Almost Black'
- 'Black Knight'
- 'Alisa'
- 'Old Times'
- 'Miss Willmott'

- 'Prima Donna'
- 'Albutt Blue'
- 'High Scent'
- 'America'
- 'Cream Eggs'
- 'Dorothy Eckford'

OPTIONS FOR PLANTING GARDEN SWEET PEAS

You don't have to be a flower farmer to grow gorgeous sweet peas, and
you don't have to plant them in long, straight rows. Your first instinct
may be to build a raised bed to accommodate your newfound friends,
but I challenge you to think about what you already have established.
You may actually find it more rewarding to utilize your existing garden
space. Could you tuck in a few sweet peas beside an existing fence or
trellis or even a column or pillar? What about trying a nontendril or
dwarf variety in a pot or hanging basket? When planted in your existing
landscape, sweet peas have this incredible ability to make you feel like
they've been there forever. Whether peeking through a patch of perennials or entwining themselves with a climbing rose, sweet peas readily
adapt to any surroundings. You likely have several existing spots in your
garden that would be perfect for sweet peas. Here are a few to consider.

FENCE

When considering where to plant your sweet peas and taking into
account their height, the most obvious, logical choice is a fence, which
will give them the stability and support they need. Chain link, wood,
or hog wire fencing paired with T-posts are all serious contenders.
Sweet pea vines can wrap around almost any structure. If aesthetics are
holding you back from using a particular surface, keep in mind that it
honestly doesn't matter what it looks like, as once those vines get going
you'll no longer see it.

ARBOR

Another great option for growing garden sweet peas is an arbor. That's one of my favorite ways to grow sweet peas, whether it's an existing arch over a garden gate or a panel of hog wire fencing bent to span the aisle between two raised beds. I also love planting them at the base of an old climbing rose and watching the magic unfurl as the two plants grow into each other. Sweet peas and roses together are pure magic.

POTS

One of the most versatile ways for gardeners to grow sweet peas is in pots. There are so many options available, and using this method allows those with even the smallest deck or terrace to experience the magic of sweet peas. Pots are perfect for showcasing not only the dwarf varieties but also the Spencer varieties. Adding a decorative obelisk or creating a simple tepee structure with just a few bamboo poles and some twine will provide enough support to try your hand at some climbing varieties as well. Pots allow you to layer your sweet peas, add various heights and dimensions to your landscape, and move your plants as needed. For example, if you have a deck and want to grow sweet peas but you think they will get too hot in the afternoon sun, put a pot on a wheeled tray to easily roll the plant to the safety of afternoon shade when necessary. For those with limited space and resources, sweet peas don't have to be a distant memory; try growing yours in pots.

OBELISK

If you're looking for a different way to feature your sweet peas, try an obelisk. An obelisk is a tall four-sided structure that narrows to a pyramid shape on top. Often used in ornamental gardens, obelisks make an outstanding support for sweet peas. They add height and dimension to your garden and can be tucked in between existing plants with ease. Obelisks come in a large variety of designs, heights, shapes, and materials, from wrought iron to wood.

GROWING FOR CUT FLOWERS Some might not think of
sweet peas as a good cut flower, due to their relatively short vase life,
but they are one of our most popular cut flowers that we sell here at
the farm. On any given day, our customers routinely snap up all the
stems we have to offer, and their eyes often fill with tears as they bury
their noses in a bouquet of freshly cut blooms, recalling their first
flower memory, stories from their childhoods, or moments in their
grandma's garden.

Because sweet peas come in a rainbow of colors—from fiery reds and
vibrant purples, to juicy oranges, sweet peaches, pale seashell pinks,
and crisp whites—they are in high demand with designers and florists.
They instantly add delicacy, charm, and something a little extra special
when tucked into bouquets and arrangements. So, whether you're a
flower farmer or a home gardener looking to add more cut flowers to
your outdoor space, do your future self a favor and put sweet peas at
the top of your list.

You know the old saying that you get what you give? I find this absolutely holds true for sweet peas. Growing them as cut flowers can be a
bit more labor intensive than just having them in your backyard garden,
but I promise you that those beautiful long stems will take your breath
away. It won't be long before you're so mesmerized that you won't even
remember the extra steps that it took to get you there.

When growing for cut flowers, most flower farmers grow their sweet
peas in long, straight rows with plants on either side of the supports.
Although not necessary for the backyard gardener, planting on both
sides of the row allows you to grow many plants in a small area with
access from both sides for easy harvesting.

HOW TO INCREASE STEM LENGTH

For any blooms to be considered great cut flowers, long stems are an absolute must. (The longest sweet pea stem I've grown to date was just shy of 30 inches [90 cm]!) So when growing sweet peas for cutting, inevitably the first question that seems to arise is, How do you ensure long stems? I'm often asked this—and my answer is always the same: I like to show my sweet peas who's boss. Now that probably wasn't the answer you were expecting, but I've learned over my years of growing that if you let the vines get all wonky, wild, and unruly, your stems will follow suit.

While some varieties of sweet peas do boast longer stems than others, the key to longer stems is simply keeping the vines tied up to their supports. Whether securing them in a row with netting, along an existing fence line, or in a pot with an obelisk, the more taut you can keep the vines, the better. Not giving your vines direction and support can result in short and crooked stems, but when tied to their support system and shown what to do, they'll exude confidence and stand tall with an almost regal elegance. As they stretch for the sun, they will grow up and out, creating the long, straight stems that are the ultimate goal of cut flower growers everywhere.

There are various ways to tie your vines to their supports; I like to use plant twist ties to keep my sweet peas secure on the netting. By making this one adjustment to your sweet peas, you should definitely see a difference in stem length, and you'll have those gorgeous long stems you've been dreaming of.

PREFERRED TYPES AND VARIETIES
FOR CUT FLOWERS

When growing sweet peas for cut flowers, there are certain types and
varieties to keep in mind in your pursuit of that perfect bloom. The
most common type of sweet peas grown for cut flower production
is the Spencer. These are hands-down the most popular among both
growers and flower farmers, as they produce large flowers in a wide
range of colors and fragrances. These qualities, paired with their long
stems, mean florists and designers swoon over Spencers and love to use
them in fresh garden bouquets.

There are many great Spencer varieties to choose from; here are some
of my tried-and-true favorites that would make great additions to any
cutting garden:

- 'Bix'
- 'Wild Swan'
- 'Chelsea Centenary'
- 'Helen Millar'
- 'Piggy Sue'
- 'Castlewellan'
- 'Southbourne'
- 'Emma'
- 'Susan Burgess'
- 'Heaven Scent'
- 'King's Ransom'
- 'Blue Shift'

Although Spencer varieties are usually the star of the show in the sweet
pea world when it comes to cut flowers, the Early Multiflora types also
deserve attention. These early-flowering sweet peas give you a jump
start on the season—perfect for an early spring wedding—and come in
a variety of colors. Some of my favorite early-flowering varieties for cut
flowers are the following:

- 'Mammoth Navy'
- 'Mammoth Salmon Cream'
- 'Solstice Rose'
- 'Winter Sunshine Cream'
- 'Winter Sunshine Light Blue'
- 'Winter Sunshine Lavender'
- 'Winter Sunshine Opal'
- 'Spring Sunshine Blush'
- 'Spring Sunshine Peach'
- 'Spring Sunshine Champagne'

SOWING TIMING AND STRATEGY

When should you sow? That is the question. With sweet peas, timing is everything; it can really make or break your season. For new growers and gardeners, the ins and outs of fall sowing versus spring sowing can be a bit confusing. Why do some of you need to start as early as September, while others need to wait until February or March?

When you should sow your sweet peas depends on where you live, what zone you are in, and what growing conditions you have available. Do you live in a warm or cool climate? Do you have a hoop house where you can give them some shelter from the wrath of winter, or are you planting them directly outside? Understanding fall and spring sowing and adapting it for your own climate and conditions is absolutely crucial for the success of your sweet peas.

FALL SOWING If you live in a mild climate or USDA zones 8 and above, with winters that usually stay above 20°F (–6°C), you can start sweet peas in the fall, any time from late September to November. If your winter temperatures get very low—that is, if they regularly dip or stay below 20°F—I recommend planting your fall-sown sweet peas in a hoop house or greenhouse. If you plan on planting your sweet peas directly outside, completely exposed, I recommend having some frost cloth on hand, especially considering the unpredictable weather patterns caused by climate change. That way you can give them a little bit of added protection against frost damage from any dangerous dips in temperature.

Growing sweet peas over the winter has several benefits. As I've said, sweet peas like cooler temps and actually prefer to be grown cold. They have a reputation for being these fragile little flowers, but the plants are another story. Sweet pea vines can handle frost with ease; they can even be frozen and still come back stronger than ever. In fact, I've had seedlings freeze rock solid in their seed trays at 16°F (–9°C), thaw a few hours later in the morning sun, and still grow just fine; you'd never have known that anything had happened.

The winter chill will cause your plants to grow more slowly, but it will also make them stockier, which is actually what you want when it comes to sweet pea seedlings. I always tell my sweet pea school students that they want rugby players in their greenhouses. No offense to any rugby players out there, but when it comes to sweet peas you want your seedlings to be short, thick, and tough, not long, lean, and lanky. The winter cold will also make the cell walls of the plant tougher, which helps them fight off viruses and pests and gives them the stamina to weather the warm summer temperatures.

Another benefit to growing sweet peas over the winter is that they don't need to be pinched. When they're grown cold, the cooler temperatures make sweet pea seedlings branch out on their own without any additional help.

If you live in an area that gets warm quickly in spring, fall sowing gives you an advantage. Fall sowing some Early Multiflora varieties gives you the best chance of early blooms before the scorching summer sun arrives.

You may be asking, *If I missed the fall sowing window, is it too late? Am I done for the season?* That depends on your zone and climate. If you are in zone 8, you can sow your sweet peas in either the fall or late winter to very early spring. If you are in zones 9 through 10, or you experience high temperatures starting in May, I don't recommend sowing your seeds in late winter/early spring. If you wait until the late winter, there won't be enough time for flowers to bloom before the plants start to wither in the heat.

Even though there are quite a few benefits to fall sowing your sweet peas, if this just isn't in the cards for you, please don't despair! Spring-sown sweet peas are also lovely.

SPRING SOWING If you live in a cooler climate, or USDA zones 7 and lower, with temperatures that dip below 20°F (−6°C), you will need to wait and plant your seeds in the late winter or early spring. Spring sowing for cooler climates can be done anytime from January through April; where you fit within this range again depends on your local temperatures and the zone you are in. Those on the higher end of the scale in zone 7 can start seeds in January; those on the lower end will need to wait until later.

When spring sowing, the general rule is to start your seeds six to eight weeks before your last frost date. You can find your growing zone on the USDA website: Enter your zip code, find your last frost date, and calculate six to eight weeks back. This is when you should be starting your seeds.

I know it's exciting to get seeds started, and it can be easy to get caught up in what all your gardening friends are doing, but knowing the correct timing for your location and sticking to it is essential and will set you up for success. Finding the exact process that works for you, your zone, and your growing conditions may take some trial and error, but with each growing season your experience and confidence will grow too, with gratifying results.

Unlike fall-sown sweet peas, which you can start outdoors, spring-sown sweet peas in the cooler climates need to be started indoors. Sweet peas need temperatures of 50 to 55°F (10 to 12°C) to germinate. Once they have germinated and broken through the soil surface, you can move them to an unheated hoop house or greenhouse, if you have one. You don't have to have a professional setup to get your seeds going, though. Do you have a garage or shed where you can set up some growing racks? Here on our farm I start our spring-sown sweet peas in our laundry room in January, and as soon as I see green shoots, I move them out to our unheated hoop house. They stay there until I plant them out in March.

Prior to planting out, spring sowers need to pinch their plants (see Pinching, page 106). Unlike their fall-sown counterparts, which naturally branch on their own in the chilly winter temperatures they grow in, spring-sown sweet peas need a bit of a nudge to start branching. Pinching your plants encourages the development and growth of side shoots, which means more bushy growth and in turn more flowers.

DIRECT SEEDING VERSUS STARTING INDOORS I'm
sure some of you are wondering, *Can't I sow my seeds directly in the
ground?* Yes, you can, though there are many differing opinions on this.
I find it really depends on your soil, your climate, what you are comfort-
able with, and your expectations for your garden.

To provide the fertile, well-draining soil sweet peas need, you might
need to add some compost or organic material to your soil before
planting. This will give the plants enough nutrients to sustain them
throughout the season. When direct sowing, it's very important to use
properly aged compost; if it's too fresh and warm, it can cook your
seeds. You also want to have your support structure in place prior to
planting. It's cumbersome and awkward to have to work around sweet
pea seedlings to put supports in place.

If you garden in a milder climate where the ground doesn't freeze, you
can direct sow your sweet pea seeds September through November, as
follows:

1 Make holes in the soil, 1 inch (2.5 cm) deep and 4 inches
   (10 cm) apart. Add one seed per hole and cover with soil.
   If you are planting a row or multiple plants, I recommend
   making a 1 inch (2.5 cm) deep trench instead, placing the
   seeds at least 4 inches (10 cm) apart, then covering them
   with soil.

2 After your seeds are tucked in, give them a good drink. I
   recommend using a watering can or a water wand with a
   fine spray setting that can best mimic natural rainfall. Since
   your seeds are so close to the surface, this will help to avoid
   the soil eroding away and exposing your seeds.

This all seems pretty straightforward and easy, right? Well, here is where many gardeners get discouraged from direct sowing their sweet peas. After planting, you will need to protect your seeds and baby seedlings from birds, slugs, snails, rodents, and other critters. Your sweet pea seeds that you just lovingly tucked into the soil are now a tempting delicacy. In fact, I've seen entire sweet pea patches destroyed overnight, and all that's left in the morning is the carnage of empty shells lying on the surface of what should've become a dreamy garden oasis. (Garden moles don't eat seeds, but their underground burrowing and pushing up mounds can wreak havoc in a freshly seeded bed.)

Even if you are able to protect your seeds, sometimes not all of them will germinate, or some seedlings will fail to thrive for one reason or another. When you've started your seeds in trays, although this is disappointing, it's not really a big deal. But when you're directly sowing, this can cause gaps and or holes in your sweet pea patch. To hopefully avoid this scenario, you can sow more seeds than necessary, then thin out the seedlings after they germinate, but that can mean a lot of work and potential waste. That said, I don't want to deter you from direct sowing your sweet peas. If you are okay with a less-than-perfect row, or you are willing to take more risk, then I say give it a try.

I admittedly am not a risk taker. I consider our sweet pea patch here on the farm the high rent district. I want to ensure that we get the most out of our space and every spot is filled with a strong, healthy seedling. Personally, I've found that starting my seeds indoors is just what works best for us here on our farm. It can get very wet here in the Pacific Northwest, which can cause sweet pea seeds to rot and plants to drown. We also have a lot of clay in our soil, which retains moisture and does not drain well. These wet conditions can cause seeds to rot. For these reasons, I choose not to direct sow my sweet peas. If your conditions are ideal for direct sowing, test it out and see what works best for you.

In anticipation of my first year of flower farming, my husband set up a growing rack for me in our laundry room. It was nothing fancy, just a plastic garage shelving unit that he attached grow lights to in preparation for our first seeds being sown. Fast forward years later, and, believe it or not, I'm still starting seeds in our laundry room! This goes to show that it doesn't take a fancy setup, a germination chamber, or even a greenhouse to get your seeds going. Do you have a space in your garage, shed, mudroom, or sunroom, or even on a kitchen windowsill? I've even seen people turn a corner of their guest room into a seed starting station. I'm a big advocate of keeping costs low while utilizing the space that you have. This may mean that sometimes you need to be a little bit creative, but no matter what your situation is, the goal is the same: getting your seeds started growing.

When starting your seeds indoors, you can better control the growing conditions for your seedlings. You can monitor the temperature, ensure they get enough light, and regulate the soil moisture, watering only when needed, instead of watching the weather and wondering if Mother Nature is going to drown your tender little starts. If sweet pea seeds are kept too cold or wet, they can rot, and if they are too warm, they'll shoot up from the soil and bolt overnight. But with proper care, they will thrive in the controlled indoor environment, and you don't have to worry about pests.

Should you direct sow or should you start your seeds indoors? The answer is totally up to you.

IV.

GETTING STARTED GROWING SWEET PEAS

We have covered quite a bit so far, and
I hope that all of this is making sense.
I also hope that understanding the basic
principles and fundamentals that are key
to sweet pea success has made you feel
more at ease on your sweet pea journey.

Have you picked the perfect location
for your sweet peas and decided on the
best time to start your seeds? Are you
planning on setting up a fresh flower
stand at the end of your driveway, or
are you growing garden sweet peas for
your own enjoyment? If you've made
these decisions, then you're ready for
the next step.

By now, I imagine you've thumbed through
enough seed catalogs and perused
countless online seed shops to choose the
perfect varieties for your patch. Whether
you chose based on color, fragrance, or
other factors, it won't be long now before
those beautiful blooms will be greeting you
right in your own garden.

This is what you've all been waiting for
and where the fun begins. So let's get
those seed packets ready. It's time to start
getting our hands dirty. It's time to start
growing some sweet peas.

SOWING

Let's get sowing! Starting sweet pea seeds is actually quite easy, but there are some variables to think about before you put your seeds in the soil.

CONTAINERS The first thing to consider is the type of container you plan to use for your seeds. Sweet peas will grow in just about anything—a pot, a seed tray, even toilet paper rolls. (I'm not kidding about the latter; we'll cover that in just a moment!) Whatever vessel you choose, make sure it offers your sweet pea seedlings two crucial things: enough room to grow and, most important, adequate drainage.

You may have some 4 inch (10 cm) pots hanging out on your potting bench. I always keep mine just in case I need them someday. For your sweet peas, this size is actually quite perfect (and bonus, you'll be using something that you already have). Four inch pots can easily accommodate at least three sweet pea seeds per pot, and they'll give your seedlings the depth and space that they need for their roots to branch and spread.

If you're a flower farmer like me, or you're going to be growing sweet peas in large quantities, then I recommend using a seed tray. Seed trays allow you to accommodate more plants in a small amount of space. Even better, the cells allow you to keep the sweet pea seedlings separate, which is crucial when you are planting multiple varieties in the same tray.

You can buy a variety of sizes and depths at your local garden center or online retailer, and you can end up spending a lot, depending on how far down the rabbit hole you want to go. There are deep-celled root trainers, which will train your sweet pea seedlings' roots to go deep, giving them longer and straighter roots without causing them to become root bound. This is helpful, because sweet peas have a very vigorous root system—you might be surprised at how big they can get for being such a small seedling. But in my opinion root trainers are not a necessity and may not be worth the expense, depending on the number of seedlings you plan to grow.

If you want to give your roots more depth but also stick to a budget, try toilet paper rolls. Yes, you heard me right. Although it may seem odd, toilet paper rolls are an eco-friendly option that also gives your seedlings' roots more space. And these are items that all of us have at our disposal (pardon the pun). You can fill them with soil and use as a biodegradable vessel to give shelter and security to your developing seedlings. And after your seedlings are established and it's time to plant them out in the garden, you can simply plant the whole roll, which will decompose over time.

Some of you may be wondering what I use. Well, here on the farm we use 50-cell trays. My first year I used a 72-cell tray (same outer dimensions, but smaller cells), and the seedlings quickly outgrew their space. I've found that a 50-cell tray gives seedlings enough space to grow from sowing all the way through to planting time. This method has worked for us, so that is what I've stuck with over the years. We grow twenty thousand sweet pea plants a year in our sweet pea patch, and with those kinds of numbers, the toilet paper roll method wasn't exactly an option for us.

LIGHT Another critical consideration before sowing is light. Are
you putting a few pots on your kitchen windowsill, or using industrial
bulbs on a growing rack? No matter what setup you choose or what
you have at your disposal, having enough light for your sweet peas is
absolutely crucial. I always get a flood of raised hands in my sweet pea
school classes when I ask: *How many of you have had seedlings that were
wiry and lanky?* One main reason this can happen is that they don't have
enough light. Sweet pea babies are very good at telling you where they
are going and which direction they favor. These tiny green shoots will
literally point and lean into the light. You can avoid the lanky stretch-
ing and set up your sweet peas for success by giving them enough light
from the start.

SOIL Unlike some other types of seeds, sweet peas aren't that picky
about what kind of soil they are started in. I like to use Pro-Mix germination medium for all of our seedlings, but in a pinch, I've also used
regular potting soil that I had on hand. Due to their larger size, sweet
pea seeds don't require the special fine medium that tiny seeds need;
they can push through pretty much whatever medium you choose to
grow them in. I like to use slightly damp soil when sowing my sweet
peas, as it allows the water to penetrate more easily instead of pooling
up on the surface.

HERE WE GO! IT'S TIME TO
ROLL UP OUR SLEEVES AND GET GROWING

1   Prepare your soil. Lightly water your soil or growing medium, then mix it well before filling your container or tray. The soil should be just slightly damp and not too wet; too much water, and soggy soil will cause your seeds to rot and can create other issues later on.

2   Fill your containers or seed tray of choice to the top with whatever growing medium you're using.

3   Using a pencil or equivalent, make a hole 1 inch (2.5 cm) deep. If you are using a seed tray, make one hole per cell. For a 4 inch (10 cm) pot, make three holes per pot in a spaced triangle. If you are using toilet paper rolls, make one hole per roll.

4   Put one seed into each hole until all of the holes have been filled. Sometimes you'll find an extra seed or two included in a seed packet; if so, there's no harm in placing two seeds in a hole or squeezing two holes into a cell. It's not necessary, but if I'm at the end of my tray and I have a few seeds left over, I will put them in with a buddy.

5   Cover the seeds with enough dirt so the holes are no longer visible and the soil level is flush across the entire container.

6   Water the pots or tray using a watering can or a water wand, mimicking natural rainfall as much as possible so it's not so harsh as to wash away any of your freshly planted soil.

7   Place your newly planted container(s) in the well-lit area where you plan to keep your seedlings while they grow.

Now comes the hard part: We wait!

GERMINATION

When it comes to germination, the waiting is the hardest part. Even after all these years of growing sweet peas, I still check the day after I planted my seeds to see if anything has come up yet. Of course it hasn't, but the anticipation always gets the better of me. Even though the teacher in me knows that germination takes time, the grower in me always runs into our laundry room like a child on Christmas morning to see what might be under the tree, just hoping to see even the slightest hint of green poking through the soil.

We actually *do* have some potential power to speed up the germination process for sweet pea seeds. Here are a few different theories and methods to try.

PRESOAKING One popular method that is thought to speed up germination is presoaking sweet pea seeds prior to planting them. Because the seeds have a thick, hard outer coat, some believe that if you presoak them in water for twelve to twenty-four hours prior to planting, you can soften that outer coat and therefore speed up germination. However, presoaking can not only reduce the germination rate but also potentially harm the seedlings by introducing fungus and disease.

Now, there is quite a bit of conflicting information available about presoaking sweet pea seeds. And I know for some growers and gardeners, presoaking can be a bit of a ritual (some like to soak their sweet pea seeds in little jars with labels prior to planting). If you've always presoaked and it's worked for you, I understand that you may see no reason to stop.

In my own research, I've noted that neither sweet pea expert Roger Parsons nor respected New Zealand plant breeder Dr. Keith Hammett recommends soaking sweet pea seeds; in fact, both advise against it. I follow their advice, which also keeps things simple. One less step!

NICKING Another practice said to speed up the germination process is *nicking*. This can be done prior to planting; it involves using nail clippers to make a small nick or scratch in the seed coat. The intent is to allow the seed to more readily absorb water and therefore speed up the germination process. This is not necessary, but again, if this is the way you've done it in the past, then I say stick with what works for you.

CHIPPING Similar to nicking is a process called *chipping*, which involves using a sharp knife or instrument to chip away a piece of the seed coat. Importantly, this should be done on the opposite side of the seed's eye (where the sprout will emerge). This method is not very common among backyard gardeners; it's mainly used by commercial growers and breeders, and only if field-grown seed has an extremely hard shell.

On average, sweet pea seeds take ten to fourteen days to germinate, and, unlike other plants, sweet peas require rather cool temperatures to germinate. Their ideal temperature for germination is 50 to 55°F (10 to 12°C). I find that the number one mistake new growers make with their sweet peas is growing them too warm. Unlike tomatoes, celosia, or other heat-loving plants, sweet peas do not need to be babied or coddled in their infancy. You don't need to use a heat mat; in fact, I beg you, please do *not* use heat mats with your sweet pea seeds! (Once, in an online sweet pea class that I was teaching, we were discussing this very subject, and I happened to glance at the chat window to see these words frantically typed: "I'll be right back; running downstairs to take my sweet peas off of the heat mat." The attendee promptly popped up from her chair and disappeared from view. Luckily, it was perfect timing! I was able to help her prevent her entire season from being ruined before it even began.) I understand—it's intuitive to nurture and turn up the heat as if we're tucking in our seeds with a blanket (and many flower seeds do appreciate the heat). Just keep in mind that sweet peas like to be kept cool in all aspects, from the temperature required for germination to the choice of bulbs for artificial lighting. Keep anything that generates heat away from their seedlings.

Under the blank canvas of soil there is magic happening in the darkness, as your seeds wake up from their winter slumber. The hard brown ball you planted just a few short days ago has now plumped up in size. The seed coat has softened and cracked open, and the seed embryo slowly comes to life and starts to unfurl.

While these changes are not yet visible above the surface, there is one thing you must do to give your sweet peas the best start possible. For all of us, water is life, and sweet peas are no exception. During the germination process, make sure that your soil stays damp—but not too moist. If you keep the soil too wet, your sweet pea babies may rot. They can also be susceptible to *damping off*—a horticultural disease that can kill or weaken seedlings after they germinate. It most commonly occurs in cool, wet conditions. Because cool temperatures are required for sweet pea germination, wet soil is a recipe for disaster.

On the other hand, it's important that the soil doesn't dry out. Without sufficient moisture, germination may be slowed or stalled. I overhead water my trays every other day during the germination process, assess the soil regularly, and adjust as necessary.

You'll notice that I said overhead water. Unlike flowers with tiny, sand-like seeds, like poppies or snapdragons, which need to be watered from the bottom to avoid being washed away, sweet peas are the exact opposite. In fact, *bottom watering* your sweet peas can be extremely detrimental (see Glossary, page 237). If left in soupy or soggy soil, sweet pea seeds can rot very quickly, and this can happen even under the most watchful eye without your knowing it.

If your seeds are germinating in a greenhouse, hoop house, or garage, or outside your house, you'll also need to be vigilant about pests at this stage. Sweet pea seeds are a favorite among common critters; they can be uprooted by birds and rodents in the blink of an eye. How you handle that issue or prevent disaster is up to you and your situation. Thankfully, this isn't an issue for me in our laundry room. When I'm starting seeds in my greenhouse, though, I cover the tops of my seed trays with another seed tray with holes in a tight grid pattern. This lid keeps the rodents out and allows me to sleep at night without worrying about my babies.

SEEDLING CARE

Within ten to fourteen days of sowing your seeds, you should start to see some signs of life emerging from the soil. Those sweet pea babies breaking through the dirt look almost like tiny serpents as they start to open their eyes and look for the light.

These seedlings need three basic elements: the right temperature, sufficient light, and the right amount of water. This is the stage where I see first-time growers make the most common mistakes: not providing enough light, and providing too much warmth. Seedlings need plenty of light, and natural light is not always enough. If you are using artificial growing lights, make sure that the lights are not hot when placed no more than a few inches above the plants. Without enough light, sweet pea seedlings will bolt and stretch, growing inches in front of your very eyes, as if asking for help. If you are seeing your sweet serpents bend, lean, and turn toward the light, don't be afraid to adjust their surroundings to make sure that they are happy and content.

When at least 75 percent of a tray of sweet pea seedlings has emerged from the soil, I move them to my unheated greenhouse. Now that they have germinated, they can be grown cold and no longer require the 50 to 55°F (10 to 12°C) necessary for germination.

Our winters here in the Pacific Northwest are considered relatively mild, with low temperatures averaging in the low 20s°F (–6 to –4°C). Keeping our seedlings in an unheated greenhouse gives them protection and shelter, but at the same time exposes them to the cool temperatures that they crave. If you live in an area that stays mostly above freezing in the winter, you can keep your sweet peas outdoors in a sunny location, bringing them inside as necessary if temperatures dip dangerously low into single digits. Sweet pea seedlings are quite tough, and once established, they can take a frost and even hard freezes and be just fine.

If your winter temperatures are regularly below 20°F there is absolutely no harm in keeping your sweet pea seedlings indoors to protect them from frigid temperatures. Just remember that they still need to be cool. Don't put them in a warm room right next to your other seedlings or plants that require warmer temps to germinate and get established; that will only create problems.

Once you see sprouts emerge, it's important to still monitor the soil and make sure they get enough water. If you've moved your seedlings outside or into an unheated space, you will probably find that you don't need to water them as often as previously. A watering regimen at this stage can be hard to calculate; I recommend continuing to monitor your seedlings daily and watering as necessary based on how the soil feels.

While sweet peas are known to be vigorous vertical growers, at this stage your seedlings should not be tall and lanky. Short and stocky is the goal. You want beefcakes, not super models.

In these cooler temperatures, your seedlings will grow more slowly, so be patient and remember that good things take time. Most of their growth is happening in their root systems as they prepare for their long journey ahead.

BED PREPARATION

Now that your seedlings have germinated and are content and growing happily on their own, it's time to get your beds prepared for planting. This is an important step, when you will create a solid foundation for your sweet peas. In essence, you're building the home where your plants will be living, growing, and putting down their roots.

Just as when building a new house, you want your foundation strong and well-constructed. Any oversights or shortcuts taken at this stage will most likely cause problems for you down the road. Taking proper care from the very beginning will make all the difference in your sweet pea results.

Here on the farm, our sweet pea beds are 2 feet wide and 75 feet long. This may surprise some of my fellow flower farmers, but we designed these intentionally to fit in more plants. More plants means more flowers, and more flowers means more seeds. Unlike other beds on our farm that are 3 or 4 feet wide (which is pretty typical on flower farms, as this size can accommodate a wide variety of different flowers), these narrower beds work well for sweet peas, since they grow vertically and not horizontally. You could say that we get two for one in our sweet pea patch when compared with other beds on the farm. The rows are separated by 2-foot paths covered with landscape fabric to keep the weed pressure down. So the pattern in our patch is: 2-foot bed, 2-foot path, 2-foot bed, 2-foot path.

If you are a flower farmer or backyard gardener and have an existing 3-foot bed at your disposal, by all means, use it! It won't change your outcome at all.

Now that we've talked about beds and spacing, let's talk dirt.

SOIL PREPARATION Whether you are putting in brand new beds or adding to your existing landscape, the soil is an important consideration. Do you have well-draining, fertile soil; sandy, loamy soil; or soil with a lot of clay? Knowing your soil type is very helpful, as it will dictate both the type of amendments you might need to add and your watering schedule.

As I've said, sweet peas are very heavy feeders and thrive in nutrient-rich soil. If you're not blessed with perfect soil, you can still improve the environment that your sweet pea babies will be living in. For example, here on our farm we do not have the perfect mix. We have a lot of heavy clay in our soil, which can be hard to break up. When creating a new bed, we remove the grass or sod and then go over the bed lightly with a rototiller to help break up the heavy clay. This is the only time that we till our beds, but we find that it makes the dirt a lot easier for us to work. Then we add a few inches of organic compost to the existing soil and mix it all together.

Sweet peas love organic material—in fact, the more organic material you can have in their soil, the better. Whether your planting area is new or existing, adding some organic compost will make a world of difference. In our existing beds, we add 1 to 2 inches of fresh organic compost prior to planting every season, making sure to allow enough time for any hot compost to cool before the seedlings go in. If your compost is not completely cooled before you tuck your plant babies into the dirt, it can burn their roots, so complete this step at least a few weeks prior.

WATERING METHODS Water is crucial for the survival of sweet pea seedlings. How you grow your sweet peas will determine how you water and care for the plants. Watering systems can be really cheap or rather expensive, depending on how fancy you want to get.

If you're growing your plants in a long row of any kind—whether it's on a flower farm, along a fence line, or on the side of your house—you will probably benefit most from using a drip-type system. In our sweet pea patch, we use drip irrigation at the base of each plant to keep our vines hydrated. We run two lines per bed, securing the lines with landscape staples so they stay in place over the course of the season. Each drip line is controlled by a valve and fed by a main line that we hook up to a hose. The water emits from holes in each line that are spaced 6 inches apart and directed right into the soil toward the plants' roots. When plants are watered this way, there is very little that goes to waste, and we're able to water twenty of our beds at a time. I literally just turn the water on, set my timer, and the irrigation system does the rest. We usually let it run for at least two hours at a time. (I know that seems like a lot of water, but the water drips out, not flowing in a constant stream, and it needs to reach all the way down to the plants' roots.)

It's really important that you do a nice deep watering and you're not just getting the surface of the dirt wet. How can you tell if your plants are getting enough water? Poke a finger into the soil to see how the soil feels below the surface. Better yet, invest in a moisture meter that tells you what's going on at the roots. If your sweet peas are starting to look wilted, then they probably aren't getting enough water; if the vines are starting to yellow at the base, then they might be getting too much.

If you're adding sweet peas to your existing landscape or tucking them in at the base of an existing arbor, gate, or plant, your watering schedule may depend on what you already have in place. If you are growing your sweet peas in pots, hanging baskets, or raised beds, you will probably want to hand water them. I personally love hand watering, especially early in the morning while the rest of the farm is still sleeping. I find it quite relaxing, and it allows me to really see what my plants are doing. In the summer, you'll always find me with my morning coffee in one hand and my water wand in the other.

How you water is completely up to you. All that really matters is that your plants get a good drink.

SUPPORT AND NETTING

Whether you need to create supports depends on the types of sweet peas you decide to grow. While nontendril and dwarf type varieties of sweet peas do not require support, if you plan on growing any Spencers, old-fashioned, grandifloras, Semi-Grandifloras, or Early Multifloras, a good support system is an absolute must. Sweet pea vines get extremely heavy when they are at their peak.

Supports come in many different forms. If you plan to plant your sweet peas at the base of an existing chain link fence, an arbor, or a structure like an obelisk or trellis that already offers something for the vines to grab ahold of, whatever it might be, consider using what you already have on hand for your sweet peas. A hog wire fence strung between T-posts works too. Whatever route you take, keep in mind how strong and tall these vines are going to get and choose something sturdy, as it just might save you some trouble later on.

My first year of flower farming, we planted a row of sweet peas on the very edge of our newly minted flower field. We were almost giddy with excitement as we pounded our 6-foot T-posts into the ground and attached the netting. We planted our seedlings at the base, and it seemed like in the blink of an eye our vines were overtaking their 6-foot supports. We quickly scrambled for a backup plan to gain more height. With my husband's background in construction, his first thought was rebar. So he took 10-foot pieces of rebar and wired them in the elbow of the existing T-posts and attached another layer of netting, and we were back in business. In the shelter of the afternoon shade, our vines that year grew to over 11 feet. It was then, in our first year of growing sweet peas, that the support system we still use today was born.

In our sweet pea patch, down the center of each bed, we place a 6- or 8-foot T-post every 10 feet down the entire length of the bed. Next, we take a 10-foot piece of rebar and poke the end into the dirt while nesting it in the elbow of the T-post. We use wire to tie the rebar to the T-post in two or three places so it's secure. This system gives us at least 8 to 10 feet for our sweet peas to climb. But we're not done yet—now we need to attach the netting.

My second year of flower farming, I felt pretty confident going into another year of growing. I knew I had learned some really good lessons in my first season and was ready to give it another go. I increased our sweet pea offerings from one row to five (looking back now, I can see that my sweet pea obsession had already begun). With my seedlings still quite cozy in their seed trays, it was time to start putting our supports in place.

At our local garden center, I noticed they had netting on clearance, and the bargain hunter in me literally leapt with excitement. It was black netting, and my first thought was that we wouldn't be able to see it. I wasn't looking or thinking about the functionality, only the aesthetic aspect of it. I brought it home, we put it up, and the seedlings were planted. Only a few weeks later, I realized that I had made a huge mistake. The holes in the netting were way too small, and the leaves of the sweet peas couldn't weave their way through it. So I painstakingly pushed every single plant through the netting, being careful not to rip or tear any leaves as they made their way to the other side of the netting.

I'm sorry to say that was not the only issue.

As the season progressed, the vines grew with wild abandon. They were loaded with blooms, and I was harvesting buckets of sweet peas in every color imaginable. It was an incredible season, and they were gorgeous—until they weren't. One morning, I went outside to find that one of the rows had collapsed under the weight of the heavy vines. Within twenty-four hours, the other four rows followed. They all went down like dominoes.

It was heartbreaking to see my beautiful sweet peas lying on the ground, helpless. The netting was not strong enough to withstand the weight of the vines, so it just gave way. We went back and forth on whether or not we should at least try to get the vines back up in some sort of fashion. In the end, we decided that out of the lemons we would make lemonade. Even though the vines were on the ground, the roots were still intact, so all hope was not lost. We decided to let the plants go and try our hand at collecting seeds.

So yes, I've had some issues with netting. I'm sharing all of this with you so that you won't make the same mistakes. The netting and support structure that you use for your sweet peas in most instances needs to be substantial enough to hold a lot of weight so that your sweet peas can continue to provide you with stunning stems all season long.

That dreadful game of dominoes in our second season taught us some hard lessons, but we learned from that experience, made the necessary improvements, and moved on, as you do in gardening and farming. Now we've got our netting system dialed, and that bad memory seems like a distant dream. If you are a backyard gardener looking to plant just a few sweet pea plants in a pot or existing flower bed you don't have to have an elaborate setup or plant in rows like we do on the farm. You can easily create a support system using bamboo poles and bailing twine or wire found at your local garden center. There are also nontendril and dwarf varieties of sweet peas that require less support due to their short stature.

SETTING UP NETTING

SUPPLIES

Gardening gloves

Hortonova netting*

Thick tie wire**

Wire cutters

Scissors

*   Most flower farms use Hortonova netting horizontally to support their tall flowers in the field; we use it vertically to support our sweet peas. You can find it from numerous online sources or even at your local garden center. For sweet peas, we recommend using an 8-foot roll if you can find it. If not, a 4-foot roll will work just fine, but you will need to string up two rows to obtain the desired 8-foot height.

*   Tie wire of various thicknesses is available in rolls at garden supply stores or at many places online.

We have found that attaching Hortonova netting to the T-post and rebar supports works perfectly and has always given us great results. We've been using this method for years. If you are a flower farmer or are planning to grow your sweet peas in long rows, follow these simple steps to achieve the same results:

1   Cut tie wire into short lengths with wire cutters for securing the netting to T-posts, at least four per post.

2   Wearing gardening gloves, position the roll of Hortonova netting vertically next to the first T-post at the beginning of your sweet pea row, and secure the edge of the netting to the T-post with tie wire in at least four places.

3   With the netting edge securely fastened, walk the roll of Hortonova netting vertically down the bed and attach it to the next T-post, making sure the netting is nice and taut between the posts. Secure it with tie wire in at least four places.

4   Repeat step 3 until you reach the end of the row.

5   When the end of the row is securely fastened, use scissors to cut the roll of netting to the desired length. The result should be a nice taut wall of white netting secure enough even for the heaviest sweet pea vines.

PINCHING

When asked what the hardest thing about flower farming is, my answer every time is the same: pinching. By nature, I'm not a very patient person. I like to see progress. I like to see green growth. Even though I know pinching is what is best for the plants, I dread this tedious process every season.

Pinching is the process of removing the central growing tip from the plant. It can be done on many types of flowers; in fact, we pinch most of the flowers we grow here on the farm. When you pinch, you're essentially telling the plant to put more of its energy into the side shoots. This causes the plant to branch, resulting in a fuller plant with more stems and more flowers.

If you have fall sown your sweet peas and grown them over the winter, you can actually skip pinching, as your cold-grown seedlings will naturally branch on their own. If you've sown your sweet peas in the late winter or very early spring, you should pinch your seedlings. Here's how: Wait until the seedlings have at least two or three sets of leaves. Then, using scissors, floral snips, or even your fingers, cut or pinch off the top of the plant right above a leaf node. Pinching really is the best thing you can do for your plants, and before long, you'll see the side branches begin to sprout, grow, and leaf out.

SWEET PEA CUTTINGS

SUPPLIES

Scissors or floral snips

Liquid rooting hormone, any brand

A small jar or vase of water

Pot or container

Potting mix

Did you know that you can actually increase your sweet pea plant stock without needing to go out and buy more seeds? Here's how to take cuttings from your sweet pea seedlings and propagate them for even more sweet pea plants:

1   Allow the seedlings you'll take cuttings from to get a tad bit bigger than if you were just pinching them. Although you can achieve the same results with your pinched stems, it is a bit easier with longer stems.

2   Using a pair of clean scissors or floral snips, cut a 4- to 6-inch piece of stem just above a set of leaves.

3   Dip the cut end of the cutting in the liquid rooting hormone solution.

4   Put the cutting in the small jar or vase of water.

5   Place the jar or vase where it will get sunlight but not get too warm. You should start to see roots develop at the base of the cutting in ten to fourteen days.

6   When you see roots, plant each cutting in a pot or container full of moist potting mix and place in an unheated greenhouse or whatever cool location you have available, making sure they have plenty of light. Plants from cuttings should be ready to plant out in the garden in just four to six weeks.

How quick and easy is that? Taking cuttings from your sweet peas is a super cost-effective way to increase your sweet pea stock, especially for those hard-to-find varieties, all within the same growing season.

PLANTING

From those little brown seeds you lovingly tucked into the dirt just a short time ago to the beautiful green seedlings you have today, you and your plants have come so far. Now that your beds are prepared and your supports are in place, it's time to move your sweet pea seedlings from their trays, pots, and containers to their permanent home in the big wide world.

When exactly you plant your seedlings outside will, again, depend on your climate and growing zone. Here on the farm, our last frost date is generally around April 15, so we plant seedlings outside in early to mid March. Remember, sweet peas can take a freeze and handle frost like a champ. When they have been grown cold, they should be able to handle both with complete ease.

SPACING The general rule of thumb with sweet peas is to allow 4 to 6 inches of space in between the plants. When spacing your seedlings, you also want to be aware of their support structure. Seedlings should be planted as close to the base of their support system as possible. Whether you are using netting, a fence, or a tepee pole system with twine, your seedlings need their supports close by as they start to reach and climb. If you plant them too far away from their supports, it can cause strain at the base of the plant when the vines get heavier as the season progresses. We plant our seedlings in two rows per bed, one row on either side of our supports and netting, with about 6 inches of space in between the rows.

As a cut flower farmer, you want as many stems as you can get. So one year I decided to try a little experiment and throw all the plant spacing rules out the window. This actually surprised me a bit, as I'm not necessarily a risk taker by nature, but I wanted to squeeze as many flowers as I could into a small space. I planted one bed of seedlings all in a row right next to each other, no spacing. My seedlings were literally packed shoulder to shoulder with just the slightest space in between. They did beautifully and didn't seem to mind their tight quarters one bit. The vines grew thick and created these massive green walls that you could literally get lost in. A labyrinth of lush green growth and whimsical stems dancing in the breeze; it was everything!

Although even suggesting this goes against all the recommended plant spacing guidelines, please don't judge me for saying that if you are growing your sweet peas as cut flowers or just to have them in your garden, you can fudge the spacing a little bit. You don't need to have a ruler at the ready and meticulously measure the distance between the plants.

If you are growing your sweet peas for seed production, then you have a little less leeway. Sweet peas will produce more seed when given space to breathe. Air flow is crucial for seed production, as it gives the plants a chance to spread their wings instead of being tied up tightly in a quest for those desirable long stems. Seed growers will see better results and higher yields if they adhere to the general spacing guidelines.

SWEET PEA SCHOOL

TRENCH STYLE SYSTEM VERSUS INDIVIDUAL
HOLES Now that it's time to plant your seedlings, there are two
approaches you can take. If you are planting only a few sweet pea plants
in pots or in your garden, I recommend digging individual holes. The
process for this is straightforward: dig a hole 8 inches deep and large
enough to accommodate your sweet pea seedling.

If you are planting quite a few sweet pea seedlings in straight rows,
I recommend using a trench system. Using a garden trowel, dig a trench
8 inches deep down the entire length of the bed. When planting larger
quantities of plants, like we do here on the farm, this method is a lot
more effective and efficient than digging all of those individual holes.

COMPOST TREAT With your trench or holes dug, I'll share with
you one of my top secrets for growing great sweet peas. I've noted that
sweet peas are very heavy feeders and love organic material. So now,
having worked organic compost into your soil, we're going to prepare
a compost treat for your plants to enjoy.

Before you plant your seedlings in the space you just dug, put a bit of
organic compost at the bottom of the prepared hole or trench. Again,
make sure the compost is cool. This essentially creates a little compost
treat or extra pocket of food for your plants, ready and waiting for when
their roots start to get established. This will also give them the added
boost they need and should provide them with enough nutrients to
support them all season long.

Cover the compost lightly with a little bit of garden soil before adding
the seedlings. Place each seedling in a hole and fill the remainder of the
hole with dirt so that it's flush with the rest of the bed. That's all there is
to it. Now all you have to do is watch and wait!

V.

PLANT CARE AND MAINTENANCE

After your seedlings are planted, it will take a while before you start to see any new growth happening. As your seedlings are getting settled into their new homes, all the growth is happening in their root systems beneath the surface. I know that, similar to the germination process, it takes time, but it's hard not to let the excitement and anticipation get the better of me.

It is completely normal to not see any changes for weeks—or in some cases, depending on the weather, to see a touch of yellowing in the seedlings. I'd be lying to you if I said that the grower in me didn't panic just a bit every year during this stage. The pressure of being what some have dubbed "The Sweet Pea Queen" can cause a little bit of angst. *What if my plants fail? Did I kill them? Why aren't they growing?* It's almost like I have one character on one shoulder telling me everything is going to be fine, and one on the other shoulder who is completely freaking out. All of these doubts, questions, and emotions are completely normal, and I'm here to tell you everything *is* going to be just fine. In fact, it's going to be more than fine: Your sweet peas are going to be great.

It will take at least a few weeks before you really start to see a change happening, but when you do, it's almost like a switch has flipped. Your sweet peas are now off to the races. Just like when children no longer look like the babies they used to be, the same is true for your sweet pea seedlings. Almost overnight, they have turned into full-fledged plants. The deep, rich, vibrant green vines start to branch and fill out, exploring the big wide world around them.

COMPOST TEA

When your vines reach about a foot tall, give them another little boost. Sweet peas don't generally like to be sprayed, but I find that if it's done correctly with compost tea, they not only don't seem to mind it—they love it.

Compost tea is a foliar feed used on most flower farms that provides nutrients to all sorts of cut flower crops. More compost, you ask? Yes, sweet peas are very heavy feeders, and when you satisfy their enormous appetites, they will respond in the most glorious way. You feed them, and they in turn will feed your soul.

There are all sorts of brewers, microorganisms, and additives out on the market to make the perfect compost tea mix. In my first year of flower farming, I loved the idea of compost tea but just couldn't justify the cost of a fancy brewer, especially since the farm hadn't seen a profit yet, so I decided to improvise and do it my way.

In my quest for a cheaper option, I discovered a product online called Bu's Brew compost tea bags. I quickly added it to my cart, and a few days later I was ready to brew.

I took a 5-gallon bucket, filled it with water, and threw in a compost tea bag. Within a few minutes, the bag started to sink to the bottom. Using an old broom handle, I gave it a good stir and then let it steep. Since I didn't have a bubbler for aeration, I went back to the bucket every hour and gave it another good stir. Eight hours later, it was ready. I added a splash of liquid kelp and a splash of liquid fish fertilizer, gave it one last good stir, and poured the most foul-smelling liquid I've ever smelled into my backpack sprayer.

I always say you can officially consider yourself a flower farmer when you've experienced splashback in the face while using liquid fish fertilizer. I can already hear the flower farmers laughing and nodding their heads at this statement. It's nasty stuff, but the plants *love* it!

HOW TO APPLY COMPOST TEA

1 When your sweet peas are about 1 foot (30 cm) tall, you can start spraying them with compost tea. Using a backpack sprayer in the late evening hours, lightly mist the entire plant with compost tea. You can also mist the soil if you wish, but it's not necessary.

2 Make sure that the tea does not pool on the leaves, as it can burn them in the sun. You want to just lightly mist and not completely drench your plants.

3 Apply compost tea every two weeks from the time that your vines are 1 foot tall, and stop immediately when you see your plants starting to set buds.

The process of spraying compost tea on your sweet peas is actually pretty simple and straightforward, but there are some strict guidelines to follow to avoid damaging the vines and creating heartache for you and your plants.

- Spray compost tea only in the late evening right before you go to bed. The worst time to spray is in the morning or mid-afternoon, letting the vines get cooked in the afternoon sun. If you spray at the wrong time, the compost tea can actually fry the vines. I learned this one the hard way. When you spray right before bed, you're working in tandem with Mother Nature and allowing the evening dew to work in your favor.

- Avoid letting the compost tea pool and collect on the leaves. Any compost tea that has collected on the cupped sweet pea leaves can burn them. If you see any liquid on the plants in the morning, promptly shake it off before the sun heats up.

- Do not spray if you see buds starting to form on your plants. I cannot stress this one enough. If your plants are starting to set buds and you apply compost tea, this boost of nitrogen will actually cause them to drop their buds; thus you'll lose all of your flowers from the first flush. I learned this one the hard way too, and it was heartbreaking!

Whether you have a compost tea brewer at your disposal or a 5-gallon bucket, using compost tea as a foliar feed at the right time of the growing season can be extremely beneficial to your sweet peas.

CORRALLING

As your sweet peas climb higher and higher, reaching for the sky, eventually they will probably need more support than the netting can give them (depending on your varieties and growing methods). Particularly for flower farmers and gardeners with long rows of sweet peas, without additional support at some point your plants will get so tall that they will flop over and possibly break. In their prime, sweet peas can grow over a foot a week, so before this happens, you will want to choose a method to give your plants added support.

Here on the farm we use a form of support called *corralling* (see Glossary, page 237). It works well with sweet peas as well as dahlias and other cut flowers that need to be harnessed and reined in. Corralling allows you to secure many plants all at once without having to tie every individual vine. You can use bailing twine, string, rope, or jute to corral your plants, following these steps.

HOW TO CORRALL YOUR PLANTS

1 Lift any fallen vines so they are all upright.

2 Starting at the beginning of the row, knot the twine to the T-post.

3 Run the twine down the bed to the next T-post, making sure to keep it taut (as you did when installing the netting). Tie the twine to the T-post and secure it with a knot.

4 Repeat step 3 until you reach the end of the bed. If you are growing plants on both sides of the netting, this process will need to be done on both sides of the row to keep the plants in place.

5 Repeat this corralling process two or three times as the vines grow.

Unless you plan on tying your sweet pea vines (see next section), they will likely need to be corralled several times at higher and higher points throughout the growing season.

METHODS OF TYING If you are growing just a few plants or have your sweet peas in various places in your landscape, you might benefit from tying your plants instead of corralling them. It is quite simple to do, especially if your sweet peas are planted in a pot or growing along an existing trellis, arbor, or fence.

I use tie wire to tie my sweet peas; during sweet pea season you will find it attached to my toolbelt whenever I'm at work on the farm. To tie my vines, I push a piece of twist tie wire through the netting, loop it around the vine, and twist the ends closed.

One added benefit of tying your sweet peas is that it can help increase stem length (see page 64). If you are yearning for those long straight stems, then tying your vines will go a long way in helping you achieve your goal.

PESTS AND DISEASE MANAGEMENT

When thinking about our gardens, we instinctively dream about perfectly green plants and handfuls of gorgeous, long-stemmed flowers, but rarely do we think about the things out there that can bring a beautiful garden to its knees. When we plant our seedlings, we're already envisioning what they'll look like at 6 feet tall. We're not thinking about the flock of birds perched in the tree watching you plant your seedlings, just waiting for you to turn your back so that they can start ripping them out of the ground. Or the slugs, silently waiting in the wings for the cover of night to fall so they can come and raid your seedlings like at an all-night buffet.

I know pests and disease aren't very glamorous or fun to talk about, but if you're not prepared and don't know the signs to look for, pests and disease can take your garden from stunning to sickly, sometimes in a matter of days.

Let's dig into the good, the bad, and the ugly so I can give you all the tools you need to handle whatever might be thrown your way.

BUD DROP One of the most heartbreaking situations you can encounter when growing sweet peas is a phenomenon called bud drop. Have you ever had stems loaded with beautiful buds one day, and the next day you see bare sticks with no buds in sight? If so, you've experienced bud drop.

Please don't take it personally; it's nothing that you did wrong. Bud drop is caused by fluctuations in temperature in the growing environment. It can also be caused by too much nitrogen or fertilizer in the soil, or by drought or inadequate watering, but mostly it's completely beyond your control. Once buds have dropped, new ones will not form, so you can just cut out those stems. The plants will continue to grow through nature's fluctuations, and as soon as the temperatures even out, new buds should no longer be affected.

SLUGS One of the biggest enemies of a sweet pea patch (especially here in the Pacific Northwest) is the slug. Slugs consider sweet pea seedlings one of their favorite delicacies, and they can literally wipe out your plants overnight. Even a single slug can cause massive damage to your seedlings in no time at all. During the day they hide—under landscape fabric and pots, in the grass—and bury themselves at the base of other plants to keep cool, only to emerge after nightfall.

To combat slugs, immediately after I finish planting my seedlings, I sprinkle a layer of Sluggo Plus in all of my sweet pea beds. Sluggo Plus is safe for our farm animals and seems to do the trick and keep the damage minimal. I keep on top of this religiously during the early part of the season and reapply as necessary.

You can also trap slugs by putting aluminum pie pans full of beer in your sweet pea patch. Slugs will be drawn to it like a moth to a flame, and let's just say it doesn't end well for the slugs.

Other options that you might have at your disposal are applying diatomaceous earth or mixing coffee grounds or nutshells in your soil.

APHIDS Truth be told, in my other flower crops here on the farm, if I see a stem covered with aphids, it actually doesn't bother me too much. I figure if I leave them alone they'll stay nice and happy where they are and not start looking for other areas of my field to call home. I do keep a watchful eye on them, though, and if they start to spread, then I treat them as needed. When it comes to my sweet peas, though, aphids are my arch nemesis, and I will absolutely not tolerate them.

Aphids come in a lovely array of colors (hopefully you sense my sarcasm?). They can be green, various shades of brown, almost black, or albino white. Once you see one aphid, you already have an issue, but if you know the early signs of what to look for you can start treating them right away before you're dealing with an overnight infestation.

The first sign that aphids have moved in is sticky sap on leaves. It is clear and glossy, easy to miss with the naked eye, but if you're like me and you know it's just a matter of time every season, then you're already on the lookout. At that first sign, I take action. Here are some products I recommend and ways that you can treat aphids in your sweet peas:

- *Ladybugs.* Ladybugs are like little soldiers in the garden, marching their way to defeat the enemy. They treat for pests and attract other beneficial insects to your garden. For best results release ladybugs in the evening.

- *Dish soap.* In a spray bottle, mix two to three teaspoons of mild dish soap with a few ounces of water. Shake well and spray on your plants. The dish soap will dehydrate the aphids without affecting your plants.

- *Safer Insect Killing Soap.* This can be purchased at any garden supply store. Apply to affected vines, following the directions on the bottle.

- *Bug Buster-O.* This concentrate can be mixed with water and will definitely be the end of your aphids. Apply to affected vines, following the directions on the bottle (though I recommend applying a slightly lighter dilution than they recommend).

No matter what you choose or how you decide to treat aphids in your sweet peas, always remember to spray only in the evening hours to avoid scorching your vines.

COMPANION PLANTING Another way to combat garden pests is companion planting. Companion planting involves being strategic in planting and placing other plants and vegetables around your garden to deter pests. This practice doesn't apply only to sweet peas; you can use it in all aspects of gardening. You can use it in your rose garden or veggie patch too; no matter the plant, the principle is still the same.

For example:
• Mint deters aphids.
• Dill attracts ladybugs that eat aphids.
• Garlic/onions deter many insects.
• Nasturtiums deter aphids.
• Ornamental alliums deter aphids and thrips.

By now you know that I love a good experiment, and companion planting is something I'd always wanted to try. In a recent season, I planted some raised beds at the end of the left side of our sweet pea patch. I planted garlic, flowering alliums, onions, dill, mint, and nasturtiums just to see how well they prevented pests in my sweet peas. Let's just say, by the end of the season I was completely sold on companion planting! I didn't see any aphids in the entire left-hand side of the patch, closer to the bed, all season long. The right-hand side of the patch was another story. I was so pleased with the results that I've started companion planting on both sides of our sweet pea rows. Hopefully the aphids will get the hint to go somewhere else; they are not welcome here!

MOSAIC VIRUS We've talked about the most common pests; now let's talk about disease. The most prevalent disease that affects sweet peas is the mosaic virus. Mosaic virus can harbor itself in various plant species, and if not detected and disposed of quickly, it can wipe out your sweet pea patch in record time.

Knowing the signs of mosaic virus will better prepare you so if you do see it someday, you'll know what to do. It usually presents with what appears to be bubbling and contorting of the foliage, like small blisters under the plant's skin. Your once beautifully cupped sweet pea leaves will start to twist and turn as if under a witch's spell. You will also notice yellow spots and streaking on the leaves and foliage. Mosaic virus affects not only the foliage but the flowers too. It's easy to tell if a flower comes from an infected plant, as the color will be off. Usually the flower will be spotted and streaky, almost as if it's been painted or dyed. When compared to other healthy vines in your garden, if something looks off with one of your sweet peas, odds are it's mosaic virus.

Mosaic virus is spread from plant to plant by insects, including aphids, thrips, and other garden pests. All it takes is one little bite and the whole plant is infected. If you see a plant that looks sick in your garden, there is no need to panic; just err on the side of caution. When in doubt, get it out.

When removing a sick plant from your garden, make sure that you sterilize any tools you use to cut the vines, to prevent spreading to other plants. I know pulling plants from your garden or patch is disheartening, but it's better than losing all of them. Mosaic virus will spread quickly, taking out everything in its wake.

Unlike mosaic virus in dahlias, which affects the entire plant including its tubers, mosaic virus in sweet peas does not affect the seed. Although it's unlikely that an infected plant will produce quality seed, the virus will not be transferred to its offspring.

VI.

HARVESTING AND SEED PRODUCTION

For me, there is nothing better than when the sweet peas are in full swing and I'm harvesting buckets and buckets of beautiful blooms. From the crispest whites and pretty pinks to bold blues and juicy oranges, I get completely lost in the sea of color. This is what I dream about all season long and when all the hard work pays off. This is when I can truly immerse myself in the beauty of sweet peas, slowly strolling down the rows while taking in their incredible beauty and intoxicating scent.

Harvesting flowers is the ultimate goal of every flower farmer and every cut flower gardener. After all the love and care you put into your seedlings, seeing your stems burst into bloom is the greatest reward for all your hard work. Whether you plan on keeping your stems for yourself or sharing them with others, you'll want to take certain steps to ensure the quality and success of your stems.

WHEN AND HOW TO HARVEST

When it comes to harvesting your flowers for cut flowers and arrangements, pay no attention to the pictures that you see on social media,
in magazines, and on those dreamy flower websites. Sweet peas, dahlias,
zinnias—most cut flowers for that matter—photograph better when
they are what we in the cut flower world call *fully blown.* This means
that the flower is completely open—and no longer a marketable cut
flower. These photos can create confusion for new growers when trying
to decide when to cut their stems; if you try to copy the look, you will
more than likely end up with some not-so-satisfied customers. Instead,
you want to make sure that each sweet pea stem has one or two closed
or cracked buds at the tip before you cut. This will ensure the longest
vase life for your flowers.

Sweet peas should always be harvested during the coolest part of the day, whether that's early in the morning or as dusk settles in. Never harvest sweet peas in the heat of mid-afternoon, and never leave fresh stems in a bucket or jar out in the sun as you keep cutting; their delicate petals will wilt in no time. Store your cut sweet peas in a cooler or refrigerator immediately after harvesting.

Sweet peas are cut-and-come-again flowers, which means the more you cut them, the more they produce more flowers. And to keep your sweet peas from starting to set seed, you need to keep cutting them.

Harvesting sweet peas is a cinch. Simply follow the stem down from the flower to the base and, using floral snips, cut where the stem branches out from the vine. That's all there is to it!

Cut sweet peas are the most requested flower at our farm stand. Our customers anxiously await their arrival every June, and it's not long before I'm left with empty buckets of water. I could honestly spend all day cutting handfuls of sweet stems; for me, being in the flowers never gets old. It's why I do what I do, so that I get to share these incredible flowers with you.

VASE LIFE The only downside to sweet peas is that unfortunately they don't have a very long vase life—typically three to five days. But there are some things you can do to get the longest possible vase life from your sweet peas. Unlike some cut flowers, sweet peas can't be stored in a cooler for days before you sell them. You want to always make sure you're using or selling your flowers immediately after harvesting, so you or your customers get the freshest product with the longest vase life. I always tell my customers that to get the most out of their sweet peas, they need to keep them in a cool or shady location in their home, in cool water refreshed daily. If possible, it's best to store them in the refrigerator at night. All of these things will keep your sweet peas looking their best for as long as possible.

SWEET PEA TENDRILS Sweet pea flowers are extremely versatile, but there is so much more to them than just beautiful blooms. Their wild and whimsical vines and tendrils have become a favorite in the flower world as well. I love using their greenery in arrangements just as much as I love using the flowers. Although I'm reluctant to cut the actual vines themselves after all the hard work of cultivating them, I'm happy to use the tendrils as a stunning addition to bouquets and arrangements, adding that pop of something unexpected and different. So when you're harvesting your sweet peas, don't be afraid to cut a little bit extra and use that little handful of stems to great effect.

GROWING FOR SEED

If you're interested in trying to collect seed, sweet peas are a great place to start, as they're one of the easiest flowers to grow for seed. As the season progresses and the temperatures warm, sweet pea flowers left on the vine will start setting seed on their own, signaling that the end of their blooming time is near and it's time to start getting ready for the next generation.

Whether you are growing sweet peas for their beauty in your garden or harvesting to use as cut flowers but also wanting to save some of your own seeds for next year's patch, the process for letting the flowers go to seed is the same: just stop cutting them. To produce seed, the blooms need to have time to mature on the vine, allowing the petals to fall off and be replaced by seed pods. Sweet peas by nature know what to do, so just walk away and let them do their thing.

I've mentioned that sweet peas are *selfers*, which means that they self-pollinate. When growing sweet peas for seed, there is no worry that any of your varieties would cross-pollinate. In layperson's terms, if you grew 'Bix' and collected seed from the plants, the seed you collected would also be 'Bix', the same as its parent.

So unlike other flowers—like zinnias, cosmos, and celosia—that must be isolated from each other so they don't cross-pollinate, different sweet pea varieties can be planted right next to each other without ever causing an issue. You just need to be careful that the vines don't get entangled with another variety so you could inadvertently combine their varieties' seeds. If you want to create a mix, this is fine, but when growing for seed, especially if you plan on selling your seeds, you should always keep your varieties true and separated. As a seed grower, I want to make sure that my customers are getting the varieties they order, and the seeds in each little seed packet are true to variety. (Of course, every once in a while there might be one in the packet that isn't correct— it happens to the best of us!) To accomplish this, at planting time, we leave a small space between varieties so their vines do not cross into another's space, and we remain extremely diligent about keeping those vines on the edges tied upright and tight so they stay within the boundaries of their variety.

We also actively *rogue* our varieties (see Glossary, page 237). The process is quite simple: Over the course of the season, carefully observe the varieties you are growing, and pull out any incorrect plants that don't belong. For example, you don't want any purple flowers mixed in with your blush, or red flowers mixed in with your blues. Cut out the rogue plant in sections, rather than trying to yank the whole plant out at the base. In most cases, you will also want to remove the roots of the imposter plant. Especially since sweet peas are vigorous growers, if the roots are left in the ground, that same purple or red sweet pea could be popping up again in no time.

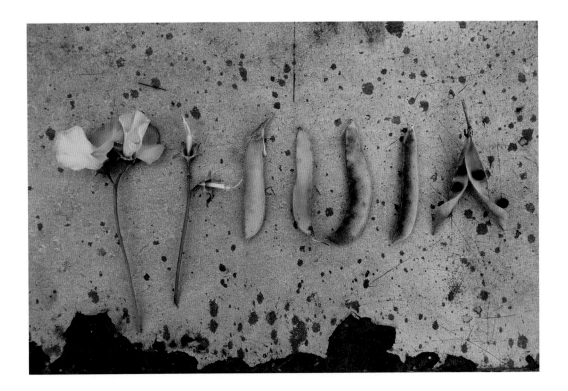

Believe it or not, most sweet pea seed growers rarely cut their flowers at all. They might cut a few for photos to use on their website showcasing the variety, but for the most part, they don't cut any stems unless they absolutely have to. This is the truth behind the more traditional "growing shots" you see on websites for sweet peas. For every flower that is cut, a seed pod is lost. From a cost perspective, that charming little vase of flowers runs you a pretty penny when you think about how many seed pods could've been.

Due to import and export restrictions, it's becoming harder and harder to get sweet pea seeds from overseas. There are only a few seed companies willing to ship seeds internationally, and with that can come some risk. Because sweet peas are technically classified as a legume (plants that produce seeds in pods), there is a chance that your seed shipment could get confiscated by customs. Every country has its own strict rules governing the importing and/or exporting of any plants, seeds, or agricultural products. So before you purchase, I recommend doing a little research to avoid disappointment when an empty seed envelope arrives in your mailbox.

The seeds of today are the promise of tomorrow's garden. Saving your seeds is also a great cost-effective way of giving yourself a head start on next year's garden. As you probably already know, sweet pea seeds are not cheap, and saving your own seeds is a great way to save yourself some money too.

HARVESTING SEED Whether or not sweet peas successfully germinate the following season depends on whether they have been harvested correctly. If harvested when they are too green, the immature pods will either shrivel in storage or not be viable. If left on the vines too long, the pods will pop open on their own, shooting the seed in every direction, and then all is lost.

Before harvesting, carefully examine the seed pods. Immature sweet pea seed pods will still be green and have a light oily or greasy feel. If you rub them between your fingers, you will be able to see an oily sheen on your fingertips. If you are still seeing greasy green pods on your sweet pea vines, these pods are not yet ready to be harvested.

Seed pods ready to harvest are brown, with a dry, tough exterior. You can lightly scratch the surface of the pod with your fingernail; if it sounds like sandpaper, it's ready to be harvested. Don't be afraid to pop a few pods open to see what's happening inside. You want the seeds to look like little round brown balls, just as they did when you first planted them all those months ago.

When harvesting my seeds, I like to collect them in large paper bags. Any breathable container works, as long as moisture can escape and won't get trapped inside, which can cause the seeds to mold. I carefully label each bag with the variety to be stored inside. I harvest straight from the vine, pulling each pod off the stem and into its bag. When I'm done harvesting that variety, I make sure to carefully fold over the top of the bag so the seeds can't escape and or mix with other nearby varieties. When a sweet pea pod cracks open due to heat and maturity, there can be great force behind it, and the seeds can travel a considerable distance. So close up your container to be safe.

Sweet pea seeds mature at different rates, depending on the weather, what stage they are at, and the variety or type. Some varieties produce more seed than others, and some produce very little seed no matter what kind of care you've given them.

When it's harvesting season here on the farm, I harvest every variety every day or every other day so I can catch every single seed pod at just the perfect time. For this seed grower, it's distressing to be working out in the patch in the hot summer sun and hear the dreaded cracking of a pod in the distance, knowing that I missed one. With twenty thousand plants each season, it's of course going to happen, but harvesting on a regular basis can help keep waste at bay. After harvesting, I allow the seeds to dry for at least a week inside our greenhouse before storing them in a cool, dry location.

When the entire harvest is complete, it is time to clean your seeds and remove them from their shells. For most of you, that means shelling by hand, but if the size of your operation and the quantity of seeds you are working with demand it, you could use a winnow wizard or seed cleaning machine. As you remove seeds from the pods, check each one for quality. Discard any that are small, undeveloped, lightly colored, or grossly misshapen. If you see just a tiny bit of shrivel here and there, for the most part that shouldn't be an issue; it just means the seed was harvested a bit too soon. If the seeds are completely concave on the sides, discard them. You should also remove any residual parts of tissue that might be left from the plant. The desired result for your sweet pea seeds is perfect little dark brown balls.

SEED STORAGE Once the sweet pea seed harvest is over, and
your seed has been cleaned and quality checked, it's time to make sure
these tiny treasures are stored properly so that all your hard work is not
lost. When stored correctly, sweet pea seeds can last for years, ensuring
that your garden will be graced with sweet pea beauty for years to come.

For long-term storage, store your sweet pea seeds in an airtight and
waterproof container. Whether it's a zip-locking bag or a plastic storage
bin, you want to protect your seeds from moisture and air at all costs.
Label each bag or bin as you go, so you know what's what. Once your
sweet peas are safe and sound inside your containers of choice, put
them in the freezer, where they can be safely stored until you need them
again for planting. If you don't have space in a freezer, use a cool, dark,
dry location where they will be protected from any pests or critters that
might find them a tasty treat.

DESIGNING WITH SWEET PEAS

Sweet peas are one of the most relatable
flowers you can grow or use in your
designs, adding nostalgia, whimsy,
and elegance to any bouquet or
arrangement. A single sweet pea stem
can elevate even the most basic handful
to something out of a romantic fairytale.
Whether used as a standalone flower in
a posy or as a supporting character in
a large arrangement, sweet peas have
incredible versatility across the floral
landscape.

MASON JAR

SUPPLIES

Mason jar

Floral snips

FLOWERS

A single variety
of sweet pea
'Castlewellan', seen left

The first arrangement I ever made as a flower farmer was a simple Mason jar of sweet peas. It will always be the arrangement that I remember the most. It brought tears to its recipient's eyes and marked the beginning of this journey for me. Anyone can recreate this uncomplicated and relatable arrangement that lets your sweet peas really shine. It's proof that sometimes the most beautiful things in life are the simplest, and often right in front of our eyes.

Simply harvest a handful of sweet peas from your garden and put them in the jar with cool water.

MIXED GARDEN BOUQUET

SUPPLIES

Floral snips

A bucket of water to place your stems in

A rubber band

Ribbon scissors

Ribbon

FLOWERS

Greenery
mountain mint
valerian
Rubus tridel 'benenden'

Large focal flowers
rose 'Bolero'
rose 'Rose Marie'

Sweet peas
'Cilla'
'Jack Eveleigh'
'Oban Bay'
'Gerry Cullinan'
'Jacqueline Ann'
'Charlie's Angel'

Additional flowers
nigella 'Cramer's Plum'
nigella 'Delft Blue'
salvia 'White Swan'
larkspur 'QIS White'
larkspur 'Misty Lavender'
silene 'Blushing Lanterns'

One of my favorite bouquets to make is the kind where I have no agenda or color palette in mind. I let the flowers speak to me, choosing what is fresh, what is at its peak. Creating a mixed bouquet is like creating a snapshot of your garden at that moment in time. In the early morning hours, I love to walk through my garden before the day's hustle and bustle begins, standing in the stillness and cutting little stems of this and that, and always a few stems of sweet peas. I find that these arrangements are the ones that mean the most to me.

1   Walk through your garden with your floral snips, collecting an assortment of stems. Place them in the bucket of water to keep them fresh.

2   Start building your bouquet by placing stems together, one by one. Turn the bouquet and spin it slightly as you place each stem, to ensure that it looks balanced and lovely on all sides.

3   When you've used all your stems, give the ends a fresh cut so they're of equal length. Wrap the ends with a rubber band, securing them in place.

4   Cut the ribbon to your desired length and tie it around the stems in a gentle knot.

BRIDAL BOUQUET

SUPPLIES

Floral snips

Floral tape

Jar or small vase with a
small amount of water

Ribbon

Ribbon scissors

Pearl pins (optional)

FLOWERS

Greenery
mountain mint
raspberry greens

Large focal flowers
rose 'Rose-Marie'
rose 'Claire Austin'

Sweet peas
'Wild Swan'
'White Frills'
'Clotted Cream'

Additional flowers
astilbe 'Bridal Veil'
tweedia
astrantia 'Moonstone'

Held by a bride on the most important day of her life, as she vows to love another forever, the bridal bouquet is the epitome of romance. By tucking in just a stem or two of sweet peas, you will not only add elegance to her bouquet but also give her an everlasting memory of the sweet delicious scent that accompanied her down the aisle on her special day.

1　Start by placing the greenery and foliage stems between your fingers in a crisscrossed pattern. This grid will help keep your stems in place while you work.

2　With a base of foliage established, place your larger focal flowers, such as roses, peonies, or lilies into their desired positions.

3　Add your other flowers to the bouquet one by one. Make sure to put your stems in at different heights to create depth and dimension in the bouquet.

4　After you have achieved your desired look, ease your fingers out of the base of the bouquet, and give all the stems a fresh cut so they are all the same length.

5　Using a piece of floral tape, wrap the base of the stems several times to secure the bouquet. Place the bouquet in water while you prepare your ribbon.

6　Cut the ribbon to your desired length.

7　Take the bouquet out of the water and gently pat dry the stem ends to avoid soaking the ribbon.

8　Wrap the ribbon around the bouquet stems to cover up the floral tape that is actually holding the bouquet together. Tie the ribbon in a decorative knot or secure with pearl pins for a more decorative and polished look.

LARGE ARRANGEMENT

SUPPLIES
Floral adhesive or putty
Flower frog
Large vase or vessel
Floral snips

FLOWERS

Greens
raspberry greens
sweet pea tendrils
Rubus tridel 'benenden'

Large focal flowers
rose 'Fun in the Sun'
rose 'Teasing Georgia'

Sweet peas
'Emma'
'Castlewellan'
'Melanie Ann'

Additional flowers
cosmos 'Apricotta'
foxglove 'Apricot Beauty'
astilbe
milkweed 'Ice Ballet'

A large arrangement or centerpiece allows you to showcase not only sweet pea blooms, in all their wild and whimsical wonder, but also sweet pea foliage. Their tendrils add texture and dimension to any arrangement with their sophisticated and understated beauty.

1   Use floral putty to secure a flower frog to the bottom of your vessel.

2   Fill the vessel three-quarters of the way with room-temperature water.

3   Place the foliage, except for the sweet pea tendrils, in the vessel to create your desired shape. Turn or spin the arrangement as you place stems at different heights to give the arrangement depth and dimension.

4   Place the focal flowers into the desired location, making sure to arrange them at different heights to create depth and dimension. .

5   Build the arrangement with the additional flowers until the arrangement is very full.

6   Add the sweet pea tendrils to the outskirts of the arrangement, which is where these subtle touches will really shine. They should drape and spill over the edges for a romantic effect.

VIII.

SWEET PEA VARIETIES

In the world of sweet peas, the range of colors and types is vast. With such a rainbow available, it can be very easy to get overwhelmed and not know where to start. In this section, I've taken out the guesswork and highlighted some of my favorite tried-and-true varieties within each color group to help you narrow down the choices. Whether you're an experienced grower looking for new varieties to add to your patch or a backyard gardener wanting to try sweet peas for the first time, this section will no doubt offer plenty of eye candy and hopefully make those selections a bit easier.

BURGUNDY/
MAROON/
RED

KING'S RANSOM

LIKE A TREASURE FROM A FARAWAY LAND or a rare gem that has been kept locked away for a very special occasion, 'King's Ransom' is a one-of-a-kind sweet pea.

This variety is a bit of a chameleon, with buds starting out as a creamy peach that intensifies with age into a rich burnt orange. In the blink of an eye, that gorgeous warm orange magically turns into a deeply rich and dusty rose. Just when you think the metamorphosis is complete, 'King's Ransom' has one more trick up its sleeve, as it once again morphs into a smoky plum.

Based on color alone, 'King's Ransom' is an unusual beauty. But its peculiar qualities extend to its shape as well. Its petals aren't flouncy and airy; they have a sturdier, almost masculine feel to them, with petals that look almost like suede. Their matte finish and intricate veining showcase their incredible range of colors.

Although I have tried my best to describe the unique qualities of 'King's Ransom', you have to see it to believe it. With blooms that stand tall on long, sturdy stems, and a delicious fragrance, this variety is a pleasure to grow.

BURGUNDY/MAROON/RED

DETAILS

BREEDER Kings

SCENT 3

TYPE Spencer

COLOR Red/Mauve

HEIGHT 6–8 ft (1.8–2.4 m)

SPACING 4–6 in (10–15 cm)

LIGHT REQUIREMENTS
Full Sun/Part Shade
(in warmer climates)

GROWTH HABIT

'King's Ransom' boasts extremely vigorous plants that, when grown in the right conditions, can reach up to 8 to 10 feet (2.4 to 3 m) tall. Plants can be either grown close together to create a wall effect or spaced farther apart if you are growing them for seed.

RENOWN

A beautiful deep crimson that shines like a jewel in the garden. 'Renown' has a richness to it with petals that look like and feel like suede.

BREEDER	Harrod
SCENT	3
TYPE	Spencer
COLOR	Crimson
HEIGHT	6-8 ft (1.8-2.4 m)
SPACING	4-6 in (10-15 cm)

ROSEMARY PADLEY

A vibrant bright red that is sure to stop you in your tracks. Perfect for adding lovely jewel tones to bouquets and arrangements.

BREEDER	Tullett/Boltons
SCENT	3
TYPE	Spencer
COLOR	Red
HEIGHT	6-8 ft (1.8-2.4 m)
SPACING	4-6 in (10-15 cm)

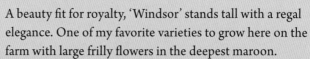

WINDSOR

A beauty fit for royalty, 'Windsor' stands tall with a regal elegance. One of my favorite varieties to grow here on the farm with large frilly flowers in the deepest maroon.

BREEDER	Brewer/Unwins
SCENT	3
TYPE	Spencer
COLOR	Dark Maroon
HEIGHT	6-8 ft (1.8-2.4 m)
SPACING	4-6 in (10-15 cm)

ADDITIONAL VARIETIES

MAHOGANY

Gorgeous deep maroon blooms on top of long, strong stems. A great option for wedding work and arrangements.

BREEDER	Hammett
SCENT	3
TYPE	Spencer
COLOR	Maroon
HEIGHT	6-8 ft (1.8-2.4 m)
SPACING	4-6 in (10-15 cm)

HANNAH DALE

Laden with richly colored blooms, this beauty has smaller flowers that look like little African violets. An incredible scent accompanies these plants.

BREEDER	Grayson
SCENT	5
TYPE	Grandiflora
COLOR	Maroon
HEIGHT	5-6 ft (1.5-1.8 m)
SPACING	4-6 in (10-15 cm)

BLACK KNIGHT

An old-fashioned favorite, 'Black Knight' boasts smaller flowers but has a wonderfully rich scent. A great addition to any garden or landscape.

BREEDER	Eckford
SCENT	5
TYPE	Old Fashioned
COLOR	Maroon
HEIGHT	5-6 ft (1.5-1.8 m)
SPACING	4-6 in (10-15 cm)

BURGUNDY/MAROON/RED

ORANGE

CLEMENTINE KISS

'CLEMENTINE KISS'—MY ABSOLUTE FAVORITE ORANGE VARIETY—lives up to its name; it appears to have been kissed by a tangerine. I love that it's not a bright, vibrant orange; it tends more toward the peach palette, and its large, juicy blooms seem to change color right before your eyes. The blooms start out as a light shade of peach and turn a dark salmon as they age. The effect is something of an ombre. Blooming atop long stems, the large flowers have just a hint of sparkle. If you love hues of sherbet, peach, and salmon, 'Clementine Kiss' is a perfect fit.

A fun and cheery flower, this variety adds a bright pop of color to design work, and its strong stems make it an ideal cut flower. It easily holds a place in my list of top ten favorite sweet pea varieties. Tracking down seeds may be a bit of a challenge, but as 'Clementine Kiss' gains in popularity, I believe it will become more available. If you're lucky enough to score some, prepare to fall in love.

ORANGE

DETAILS

BREEDER Matthewman

SCENT 3

TYPE Spencer

COLOR Orange

HEIGHT 6–8 ft (1.8–2.4 m)

SPACING 4–6 in (10–15 cm)

LIGHT REQUIREMENTS
Full Sun/Part Shade
(in warmer climates)

GROWTH HABIT

Clementine Kiss boasts vigorous plants that, when grown in the right conditions, can reach up to 8 feet (2.4 m) tall. Plants can be grown either close together to create a wall effect or spaced farther apart if you are growing them for seed.

One of my favorite varieties, this stunning early flowering variety boasts some of the longest stems I've ever seen. Large frilly blooms are the perfect orangey-peach color that pairs well with many different color palettes.

BREEDER	Owls Acre
SCENT	3
TYPE	Early Multiflora
COLOR	Salmon
HEIGHT	6-8 ft (1.8-2.4 m)
SPACING	4-6 in (10-15 cm)

SPRING SUNSHINE PEACH

This highly sought-after variety is popular for good reason. The queen of the oranges, 'Apricot Queen' is an extremely fragrant variety that has some of the most gorgeous flowers I have ever seen.

BREEDER	E. W. King
SCENT	5
TYPE	Spencer
COLOR	Apricot Orange
HEIGHT	6-8 ft (1.8-2.4 m)
SPACING	4-6 in (10-15 cm)

APRICOT QUEEN

A lovely orange variety that deserves more attention. These plants are smothered with blooms in a bright coral that will make you stop and stare.

BREEDER	Harrod
SCENT	3
TYPE	Spencer
COLOR	Orange
HEIGHT	6-8 ft (1.8-2.4 m)
SPACING	4-6 in (10-15 cm)

LEN HARROD

ADDITIONAL VARIETIES

One of the tallest and most vigorous plants in the patch, 'Edith Flanagan' has large, stunning blooms in a deep burnt orange. A wonderful variety with vibrant color.

BREEDER	Beane/Parsons
SCENT	3
TYPE	Spencer
COLOR	Orange
HEIGHT	6-8 ft (1.8-2.4 m)
SPACING	4-6 in (10-15 cm)

EDITH FLANAGAN

This fun little novelty is aptly named. A true standout in the garden, these sweet orange flowers have blue veining that becomes more vivid with age.

BREEDER	Hammett
SCENT	3
TYPE	Spencer
COLOR	Orange
HEIGHT	6-8 ft (1.8-2.4 m)
SPACING	4-6 in (10-15 cm)

BLUE VEIN

ORANGE

An heirloom variety that has graced gardens for almost a century. These tall, vigorous plants offer a bounty of bright orange blooms on long stems.

BREEDER	Morse
SCENT	3
TYPE	Spencer
COLOR	Orange
HEIGHT	6-8 ft (1.8-2.4 m)
SPACING	4-6 in (10-15 cm)

PRINCE OF ORANGE

PEACH/
APRICOT

EMMA

'EMMA', A TRUE SWEETHEART OF THE GARDEN, produces large, frilly flowers that seem to twirl in the warm summer air, almost as if dancing. I'm so smitten with this variety that I named my cat after her! Her soft salmon-hued blossoms top long, strong stems, making her an amazing cut flower. This girl really has it all, with the perfect mix of sweet citrusy fragrance and gorgeous blooms with flushed peach petals.

'Emma' is the perfect mix of femininity, elegance, and romance. She blends so well with a variety of different color palettes that she is my go-to bloom for bouquets, arrangements, and wedding work. Her perfect petals add sophistication and style to any arrangement. The only drawback to 'Emma' is that she isn't the best seed producer, which is why it can be a little hard to find seeds of this variety. I've found that she produces more seed if she's given space and the plants aren't crowded. Presently, 'Emma' is a bit of a unicorn (flower lovers' lingo for "impossible to find") in the sweet pea world, but I have no doubt that as her popularity grows, seed growers will answer the call.

PEACH/APRICOT

DETAILS

BREEDER Brackley

SCENT 3

TYPE Spencer

COLOR Peach

HEIGHT 6–8 ft (1.8–2.4 m)

SPACING 4–6 in (10–15 cm)

LIGHT REQUIREMENTS
Full Sun/Part Shade
(in warmer climates)

GROWTH HABIT

'Emma' boasts extremely vigorous plants that when grown in the right conditions can reach up to 8 to 10 feet (2.4 to 3 m) tall. Plants can be grown either close together to create a wall effect or spaced farther apart if you are growing them for seed. If growing for seed, give 'Emma' a lot of room, as she is a finicky variety that can trick even the most seasoned grower.

This gorgeous gem is tall and simply stunning. Beautiful large peach blooms have just a touch of coral and add something special to bouquets.

BREEDER	Eagle
SCENT	3
TYPE	Spencer
COLOR	Salmon
HEIGHT	6–8 ft (1.8–2.4 m)
SPACING	4–6 in (10–15 cm)

WILLIAM & CATHERINE

A breathtaking beauty that steals my heart year after year. Petals are a creamy peach that stands out both in the garden as well as in bouquets.

BREEDER	Parsons
SCENT	4
TYPE	Spencer
COLOR	Pale Salmon
HEIGHT	6–8 ft (1.8–2.4 m)
SPACING	4–6 in (10–15 cm)

YVETTE ANN

'Heaven Scent' should be a staple in your sweet pea garden. These plants are extremely tall with the most perfect peach blooms that glisten in the sun on long, strong stems.

BREEDER	Parsons
SCENT	4
TYPE	Spencer
COLOR	Pale Salmon
HEIGHT	6–8 ft (1.8–2.4 m)
SPACING	4–6 in (10–15 cm)

HEAVEN SCENT

ADDITIONAL VARIETIES

A stunning addition to any garden, these blooms are a darker peach with touches of coral and cream.

BREEDER	Harrod/Unwins
SCENT	3
TYPE	Spencer
COLOR	Salmon
HEIGHT	6-8 ft (1.8-2.4 m)
SPACING	4-6 in (10-15 cm)

JUST JANET

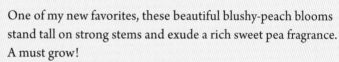

One of my new favorites, these beautiful blushy-peach blooms stand tall on strong stems and exude a rich sweet pea fragrance. A must grow!

BREEDER	Harrod
SCENT	4
TYPE	Spencer
COLOR	Peach
HEIGHT	6-8 ft (1.8-2.4 m)
SPACING	4-6 in (10-15 cm)

GILLY NORAH

PEACH/APRICOT

I will always grow 'Castlewellan' here on the farm. A stunning light peach variety with large flowers and great stem length. This variety has my heart completely.

BREEDER	Harrod/Unwins
SCENT	3
TYPE	Spencer
COLOR	Peach
HEIGHT	6-8 ft (1.8-2.4 m)
SPACING	4-6 in (10-15 cm)

CASTLEWELLAN

CREAM/
WHITE

WILD SWAN

THE FRILLIEST OF FLOWERS! In a sea of white sweet peas, 'Wild Swan' stands tall, as if it were the only one floating on the pond. A perfectly named variety, 'Wild Swan' boasts the frilliest petals I've ever seen on a sweet pea. They look like a butterfly's wings ready to take flight. These wildly elegant flowers in the purest white would be a picture-perfect addition to any bridal bouquet. Their vines are loaded with masses of big, beautiful flowers on long, strong stems, making this variety ideal to design and arrange with. If I had to pick only one white sweet pea to grow, 'Wild Swan' would be it. Not only are these flowers simply stunning, but this variety is also an incredible seed producer.

DETAILS

BREEDER Hammett

SCENT 3

TYPE Spencer, Hardy annual

COLOR White

HEIGHT 6-8 ft (1.8-2.4 m)

SPACING 4-6 in (10-15 cm)

LIGHT REQUIREMENTS
Full Sun/Part Shade
(in warmer climates)

CREAM/WHITE

GROWTH HABIT

'Wild Swan' stands tall in the garden, with extremely vigorous plants that, when grown in the right conditions, can reach up to 8 to 10 feet (2.4 to 3 m) tall. Plants can be grown either close together to create a wall effect or spaced farther apart if you are growing them for seed.

ADDITIONAL VARIETIES

A cutting garden staple and must-grow for wedding work! 'White Frills' has large, gorgeous flowers in a clean and crisp white.

BREEDER	Truslove/Kerton
SCENT	3
TYPE	Spencer
COLOR	White
HEIGHT	6-8 ft (1.8-2.4 m)
SPACING	4-6 in (10-15 cm)

WHITE FRILLS

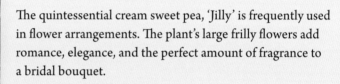

The quintessential cream sweet pea, 'Jilly' is frequently used in flower arrangements. The plant's large frilly flowers add romance, elegance, and the perfect amount of fragrance to a bridal bouquet.

BREEDER	Harriss/Unwins
SCENT	4
TYPE	Spencer
COLOR	Cream
HEIGHT	6-8 ft (1.8-2.4 m)
SPACING	4-6 in (10-15 cm)

JILLY

These lovely blooms come in the softest cream color. Long stems make them perfect for wedding work, bouquets, and cutting gardens.

BREEDER	Brewer/Matthewman
SCENT	3
TYPE	Spencer
COLOR	Cream
HEIGHT	6-8 ft (1.8-2.4 m)
SPACING	4-6 in (10-15 cm)

CLOTTED CREAM

This variety reminds me of key lime pie. The cream flowers look as if they have been kissed with the faintest hint of tangy lime.

BREEDER	Owl's Acre
SCENT	3
TYPE	Limelight
COLOR	Cream
HEIGHT	6-8 ft (1.8-2.4 m)
SPACING	4-6 in (10-15 cm)

LIMELIGHT

An antique cream color on the edge of these petals gives the blooms a vintage look and feel.

BREEDER	Chisholm/Kerton
SCENT	3
TYPE	Spencer
COLOR	White
HEIGHT	6-8 ft (1.8-2.4 m)
SPACING	4-6 in (10-15 cm)

MRS R CHISHOLM

CREAM/WHITE

A dazzling white variety with huge frilly petals that dance in the breeze. A great choice for bouquets and arrangements.

BREEDER	Eagle
SCENT	3
TYPE	Spencer
COLOR	White
HEIGHT	6-8 ft (1.8-2.4 m)
SPACING	4-6 in (10-15 cm)

LUCY HAWTHORNE

BLUSH

BIX

'BIX', A TRUE BLUSHING BEAUTY, is a real standout in the garden. 'Bix' oozes charm, sophistication, and elegance, like a true southern belle who's been raised with grace. These sweet, stunning stems are the palest shade of vintage cream with just a hint of blush around the edges that looks almost like a watercolor painting. These blooms are some of the best in the patch; they feel like they've come straight out of a romance novel, with breathtaking beauty that will win over even the hardest of hearts. 'Bix' is an early-flowering variety, which means she's always early to the sweet pea party, and if you need or want early flowers, then 'Bix' is the perfect pick for you. Florists will love this variety, with its tall, vigorous vines loaded with big, beautiful flowers on long, strong stems. 'Bix' will always be at the top of my list.

DETAILS

BREEDER Hammett

SCENT 3

TYPE Spencer, Hardy Annual

COLOR Blush

HEIGHT 6-8 ft (1.8-2.4 m)

SPACING 4-6 in (10-15 cm)

LIGHT REQUIREMENTS
Full Sun/Part Shade
(in warmer climates)

GROWTH HABIT

'Bix' stands tall in the garden, with extremely vigorous plants that, when grown in the right conditions, can reach up to 8 to 10 feet (2.4 to 3 m) tall. Plants can be grown either close together to create a wall effect or spaced farther apart if you are growing them for seed.

BLUSH

ADDITIONAL VARIETIES

One of my favorite blushes, 'Mollie Rilstone' checks all of the boxes. A lovely creamy blush color with pink edging, great stem length, and the perfect sweet pea perfume. A must grow!

BREEDER	Tremewan
SCENT	4
TYPE	Spencer
COLOR	Pink Picotee
HEIGHT	6-8 ft (1.8-2.4 m)
SPACING	4-6 in (10-15 cm)

MOLLIE RILSTONE

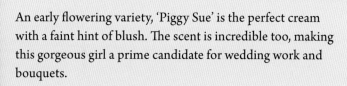

An early flowering variety, 'Piggy Sue' is the perfect cream with a faint hint of blush. The scent is incredible too, making this gorgeous girl a prime candidate for wedding work and bouquets.

BREEDER	Hammett
SCENT	5
TYPE	Early Multiflora Spencer
COLOR	Blush
HEIGHT	6-8 ft (1.8-2.4 m)
SPACING	4-6 in (10-15 cm)

PIGGY SUE

A truly splendid variety, 'Gwawr Cymru' stands tall in the garden. This lovely blush beauty will always have a place in my sweet pea patch.

BREEDER	Harrod/Parsons
SCENT	3
TYPE	Spencer
COLOR	Blush
HEIGHT	6-8 ft (1.8-2.4 m)
SPACING	4-6 in (10-15 cm)

GWAWR CYMRU
AKA WELSH DAWN

One of my favorite blushes and a showstopper in the garden. Long stems and beautiful blooms in a pretty shade of blush.

BREEDER	Eagle
SCENT	3
TYPE	Spencer
COLOR	Pink Picotee
HEIGHT	6-8 ft (1.8-2.4 m)
SPACING	4-6 in (10-15 cm)

KIERA MADELINE

A newfound favorite, 'Frilly Milly' has incredible stem length and large, flouncy blooms with a delectable fragrance. For me, it was love at first sight.

BREEDER	Hammett
SCENT	4
TYPE	Spencer
COLOR	Blush
HEIGHT	6-8 ft (1.8-2.4 m)
SPACING	4-6 in (10-15 cm)

FRILLY MILLY

Creamy white blooms with a darker pink edging make this variety just a bit different than the other blushes. These plants are vigorous and produce tons of flowers on long stems.

BREEDER	Beane/Myers
SCENT	3
TYPE	Spencer
COLOR	White with pink edge
HEIGHT	6-8 ft (1.8-2.4 m)
SPACING	4-6 in (10-15 cm)

DEBORAH DEVONSHIRE

BLUSH

SUSAN BURGESS

'SUSAN BURGESS' EXUDES CHARM AND REFINEMENT, appearing as if straight out of a Georgian era love story. I envision Mr. Darcy giving Elizabeth Bennet a handful of these sweet blooms in his attempt to woo her.

'Susan Burgess' boasts large, frilly flowers in a beautiful shade of rosy pink with hints of antique white that bring to mind the finest strawberries and cream. Her gorgeous flowers have a vintage quality, blooming on long, strong stems. This is another variety that's perfect for bouquets and design work.

The real Susan Burgess was a lovely woman who lived in England. Her daughter bought the naming rights from Roger Parsons and named this variety after her mother as a birthday present for her eightieth birthday. Susan passed away a few years later, but her memory lives on in this alluring flower.

PINK

DETAILS

BREEDER
Andrew Beane/Roger Parsons

SCENT 3

TYPE Spencer, Hardy Annual

COLOR Pink

HEIGHT 6–8 ft (1.8–2.4 m)

SPACING 4–6 in (10–15 cm)

LIGHT REQUIREMENTS
Full Sun/Part Shade
(in warmer climates)

GROWTH HABIT

'Susan Burgess' stands tall in the garden, with extremely vigorous plants that, when grown in the right conditions, can reach up to 8 to 10 feet (2.4 to 3 m) tall. Plants can be grown either close together to create a wall effect or spaced farther apart if you are growing them for seed.

Salmon-colored blooms with just a touch of cream give this plant a bit of a vintage feel. An attractive addition to any garden.

BREEDER	Albutt/Eagle
SCENT	3
TYPE	Spencer
COLOR	Salmon Pink
HEIGHT	6-8 ft (1.8-2.4 m)
SPACING	4-6 in (10-15 cm)

SYLVIA MOORE

These perfectly pink blooms dance in the garden like a ballerina's tutu. With an impressive stem length, 'Southbourne' will always have a place in my sweet pea patch.

BREEDER	Colledge/Unwins
SCENT	3
TYPE	Spencer
COLOR	Pale Pink
HEIGHT	6-8 ft (1.8-2.4 m)
SPACING	4-6 in (10-15 cm)

SOUTHBOURNE

Nora has captured the heart of so many sweet pea lovers. A delicious light pink bloom that is incredibly versatile in bouquets and arrangements.

BREEDER	Tremewan
SCENT	3
TYPE	Spencer
COLOR	Pale Salmon Pink
HEIGHT	6-8 ft (1.8-2.4 m)
SPACING	4-6 in (10-15 cm)

NORA HOLMAN

If pink is your color, put this one on your list! Pale pink blooms on a creamy white background are simply stunning.

BREEDER	Parsons
SCENT	4
TYPE	Spencer
COLOR	Pale Pink
HEIGHT	6-8 ft (1.8-2.4 m)
SPACING	4-6 in (10-15 cm)

JOHN GRAY

I absolutely fell in love with this variety from the second I saw it. An incredible soft pink that has an opalescent sheen as it glistens in the summer sun.

BREEDER	Robertson/Kerton
SCENT	3
TYPE	Spencer
COLOR	Pale Pink
HEIGHT	6-8 ft (1.8-2.4 m)
SPACING	4-6 in (10-15 cm)

LYNN FIONA

PINK

When a breeder names a variety after his wife, you know it's going to be special. These must-grow blooms exude romance.

BREEDER	Jones/Unwins
SCENT	3
TYPE	Spencer
COLOR	Pink
HEIGHT	6-8 ft (1.8-2.4 m)
SPACING	4-6 in (10-15 cm)

MRS BERNARD JONES

BLUE SHIFT

MOST SWEET PEA VARIETIES PRODUCE consistently colored blooms, but Blue Shift breaks the mold. Bred by Dr. Keith Hammett in New Zealand, it has an incredible range of colors, with no two blooms the same. Its color-changing magic is truly breathtaking. The medium-sized flowers vary from stem to stem, ranging from rich shades of purple with hints of mauve, rose, and fuchsia, to exquisite blues including navy, aquamarine, and deep electric blue. Some blooms start out purple with blue veining before fading to aqua, which is why here on the farm we lovingly refer to 'Blue Shift' as "the tie-dye flower." The vines are loaded with plentiful flowers on long, strong stems, which makes this variety perfect for growing as a cut flower or just enjoying them in your garden.

'Blue Shift' brings a kaleidoscope of color to bouquets and arrangements. It's a wonderful bridge flower that marries rich purples and blues with subtle pops of berry tones. It pairs perfectly with stock, campanula, tweedia, forget-me-nots, and nigella. 'Blue Shift' offers up a subtle, sweet fragrance, as if each bloom has been dipped in sugar.

BLUE

DETAILS

BREEDER Dr. Keith Hammett

SCENT 3

TYPE Spencer, Hardy Annual

COLOR Blue

HEIGHT 6-8 ft (1.8-2.4 m)

SPACING 4-6 in (10-15 cm)

LIGHT REQUIREMENTS
Full Sun/Part Shade
(in warmer climates)

GROWTH HABIT

'Blue Shift' stands tall in the garden, with extremely vigorous plants that, when grown in the right conditions, can reach up to 8 to 10 feet (2.4 to 3 m) high. Plants can be grown either close together to create a wall effect or spaced farther apart if you are growing them for seed.

A time-tested favorite that continues to capture flower lovers' hearts. The stunning mid-blue color makes this the perfect "something blue" for bridal bouquets.

BREEDER	Davis/Marchant
SCENT	3
TYPE	Spencer
COLOR	Mid Blue
HEIGHT	6-8 ft (1.8-2.4 m)
SPACING	4-6 in (10-15 cm)

OUR HARRY

Roger Parsons named this variety after his lovely wife and every time I see it, I think of them. Such a beautiful blue with an enchanting fragrance. A must-grow!

BREEDER	Parsons
SCENT	4
TYPE	Spencer
COLOR	Mid Blue
HEIGHT	6-8 ft (1.8-2.4 m)
SPACING	4-6 in (10-15 cm)

ALISON LOUISE

Named after the English singer Cilla Black, this lovely icy blue flower captivates. 'Cilla' boasts large, ruffled flowers and notable stem length.

BREEDER	Bell
SCENT	3
TYPE	Spencer
COLOR	Pale Blue
HEIGHT	6-8 ft (1.8-2.4 m)
SPACING	4-6 in (10-15 cm)

CILLA

A sweet pea classic, these pale blue stems are a garden staple, great for bouquets and arrangements.

BREEDER	Hanmer
SCENT	3
TYPE	Spencer
COLOR	Pale Blue
HEIGHT	6-8 ft (1.8-2.4 m)
SPACING	4-6 in (10-15 cm)

CHARLIE'S ANGEL

There's something about this variety that stops me in my tracks. Blue with just a hint of purple, these blooms are one-of-a-kind.

BREEDER	Parsons
SCENT	4
TYPE	Spencer
COLOR	Mid Blue
HEIGHT	6-8 ft (1.8-2.4 m)
SPACING	4-6 in (10-15 cm)

JUST JULIA

BLUE

The stem length on this variety is absolutely incredible—some of the longest stems I've ever seen. Combined with an eye-catching light blue flower, this beauty is a must-grow!

BREEDER	Hammett
SCENT	3
TYPE	Spencer
COLOR	Pale Blue
HEIGHT	6-8 ft (1.8-2.4 m)
SPACING	4-6 in (10-15 cm)

CHELSEA CENTENARY

GERRY CULLINAN

I DON'T USUALLY GRAVITATE toward the color purple, but that all changed when I saw 'Gerry Cullinan' bloom for the very first time. As though it just stepped out of the Victorian era, this gorgeous bloomer had me completely captivated with its romantic charm. I could see these sweet stems gracing tabletops at a traditional English tea—paired with cucumber sandwiches, scones, and biscuits on fine china—or gracing the entryway of an estate hosting the first ball of the season.

The large, frilly flowers of 'Gerry Cullinan' have glittery petals that literally sparkle in the sunlight. They are the perfect shade of lavender with an antique cream background. Stems are long, making them a wonderful addition to any cutting garden. Although not very commonly available, if you can find it this variety will become the belle of the ball.

PURPLE

DETAILS

BREEDER Kerton

SCENT 5

TYPE Spencer, Hardy Annual

COLOR Purple

HEIGHT 6-8 ft (1.8-2.4 m)

SPACING 4-6 in (10-15 cm)

LIGHT REQUIREMENTS
Full Sun/Part Shade
(in warmer climates)

GROWTH HABIT

'Gerry Cullinan' stands tall in the garden, with extremely vigorous plants that, when grown in the right conditions, can reach up to 8 to 10 feet (2.4 to 3 m) tall. Plants can be grown either close together to create a wall effect or spaced farther apart if you are growing them for seed.

MISTY

An essential for any garden. These large frilly blooms are the perfect marriage of pink and purple. Mixes well with many different color palettes.

BREEDER	Leese/Eagle
SCENT	3
TYPE	Spencer
COLOR	Pale Mauve Purple
HEIGHT	6-8 ft (1.8-2.4 m)
SPACING	4-6 in (10-15 cm)

TERRY DAVEY

A new favorite on the farm, this up and coming variety deserves a place in your garden. 'Terry Davey' boasts large, vibrant flowers and remarkable stem length.

BREEDER	Davey
SCENT	3
TYPE	Spencer
COLOR	Mauve Purple
HEIGHT	6-8 ft (1.8-2.4 m)
SPACING	4-6 in (10-15 cm)

WELCOME TO YORKSHIRE

I am absolutely smitten with this beauty. These dark purple blooms are kissed with the faintest hint of soft mauve and feel like suede.

BREEDER	Matthewman
SCENT	3
TYPE	Spencer
COLOR	Dark Mauve Purple
HEIGHT	6-8 ft (1.8-2.4 m)
SPACING	4-6 in (10-15 cm)

A tried and true favorite, these soft lavender blooms are a staple here on the farm. The frilly flowers are perfect for fresh garden bouquets.

BREEDER	Parsons
SCENT	3
TYPE	Spencer
COLOR	Lavender
HEIGHT	6-8 ft (1.8-2.4 m)
SPACING	4-6 in (10-15 cm)

JACQUELINE ANN

A stunning sweet pea with lavender blooms. Ethel has become a regular in sweet pea gardens—give her a spot in yours!

BREEDER	B.R. Jones/ Bolton
SCENT	3
TYPE	Spencer
COLOR	Lavender
HEIGHT	6-8 ft (1.8-2.4 m)
SPACING	4-6 in (10-15 cm)

ETHEL GRACE

PURPLE

'Annabelle' stole my heart. These gorgeous soft purple blooms are the epitome of romance and elegance.

BREEDER	Bolton
SCENT	3
TYPE	Spencer
COLOR	Lavender
HEIGHT	6-8 ft (1.8-2.4 m)
SPACING	4-6 in (10-15 cm)

ANNABELLE

FLAKES

RASPBERRY FLAKE

IN A CLASS ALL THEIR OWN, flakes are one of the most intriguing sweet pea types that you can grow. They not only blend well with a variety of different color palettes, making them the perfect bridge flower, but can also stand all on their own in a vase. Like a perfect summer dessert, 'Raspberry Flake' is a delicious berry color that pairs beautifully with its creamy white background. Its petals' soft streaking creates an almost vintage quality, giving you the feeling that it has graced gardens for years. This stunning variety boasts large, frilly petals that look like a bed of fanned-out coral wafting on the sea floor. Vines are loaded with plentiful flowers on long, strong stems, which make this variety perfect for growing as a cut flower or just enjoying them in your garden. This variety can be a bit disappointing for seed-savers, as it's not the best producer, but I'm sure as it grows in popularity it will become more widely available very soon.

FLAKES

DETAILS

BREEDER Unwins

SCENT 4

TYPE Spencer, Hardy Annual

COLOR Flake

HEIGHT 6-8 ft (1.8-2.4 m)

SPACING 4-6 in (10-15 cm)

LIGHT REQUIREMENTS
Full Sun/Part Shade
(in warmer climates)

GROWTH HABIT

'Raspberry Flake' stands tall in the garden, with extremely vigorous plants that, when grown in the right conditions, can reach up to 8 to 10 feet (2.4 to 3 m) high. Plants can be grown either close together to create a wall effect or spaced farther apart if you are growing them for seed.

NIMBUS

One of my favorite flakes and the most requested variety from our customers. The deep eggplant color mixes well in bouquets but also stands strong on its own.

BREEDER	Unwins
SCENT	3
TYPE	Spencer
COLOR	Dark Purple Flake
HEIGHT	6-8 ft (1.8-2.4 m)
SPACING	4-6 in (10-15 cm)

CHOCOLATE FLAKE

An exquisite, deep maroon flake that completely has my heart. If you love deep jewel tones, this variety is for you.

BREEDER	Hammett
SCENT	3
TYPE	Spencer
COLOR	Maroon Flake
HEIGHT	6-8 ft (1.8-2.4 m)
SPACING	4-6 in (10-15 cm)

SUZY Z

A distinctive maroon flake on gray ground. Suzy makes me smile. There is something incredibly rich about her blooms.

BREEDER	Owl's Acre
SCENT	3
TYPE	Spencer
COLOR	Maroon Flake
HEIGHT	6-8 ft (1.8-2.4 m)
SPACING	4-6 in (10-15 cm)

A stunning maroon stripe on gray ground with frilly petals. Deserving of a spot in any cutting garden, 'Olive D' also adds something different to fresh garden bouquets.

BREEDER	Owl's Acre
SCENT	3
TYPE	Spencer
COLOR	Maroon Stripe
HEIGHT	6-8 ft (1.8-2.4 m)
SPACING	4-6 in (10-15 cm)

OLIVE D

An amazing dark blue flake that makes a statement all on its own. I love using this variety in mixed bouquets, but a simple mason jar with just these beauties will take your breath away too.

BREEDER	McDonald/Parsons
SCENT	3
TYPE	Spencer
COLOR	Dark Blue Flake
HEIGHT	6-8 ft (1.8-2.4 m)
SPACING	4-6 in (10-15 cm)

MR P

FLAKES

This tricolor flake is truly fascinating! These large flowers are deep purple and blue on gray ground, a magical combination and a must-grow.

BREEDER	Hammett
SCENT	3
TYPE	Spencer
COLOR	Bicolor Flake
HEIGHT	6-8 ft (1.8-2.4 m)
SPACING	4-6 in (10-15 cm)

EARL GREY

GLOSSARY

{BOTTOM WATERING} giving your plant's roots hydration from the bottom up, allowing the soil to draw up water into the roots.

{COMPANION PLANTING} using a variety of plants to prevent pests and disease.

{CORRALLING} gathering plants together to provide support.

{CROSSES} new varieties created by transferring pollen from one plant to the other.

{CULTIVARS} a plant variety that has been produced by selective breeding.

{DAMPING OFF} a fungal disease that affects young seedlings causing the stem to rot at the soil line.

{FULLY-BLOWN} flowers that have opened completely.

{GENETIC DRIFT} random changes in the genetic makeup of a plant population over time due to natural selection.

{GENUS} a scientific classification, between family and species, that groups plants (or other living things) by common characteristics or traits.

{OVERHEAD WATERING} giving your plants hydration from overhead as if to mimic rainfall.

{REVERSE BICOLOR} a flower whose sepals are darker than the petals.

{ROGUE} the act of removing an incorrect variety from a group in order to keep the varieties uniform.

{SELFER} a plant that is self-pollinating and does not cross-pollinate with other varieties.

{SELF-SEEDING} reproducing and spreading by the dispersal of its own seeds, without human involvement.

{SPECIES} a type of plant having certain characteristics that differentiate it from other members of its genus.

{SPORT} a genetic mutation that has no explanation and no specific rhyme or reason for its occurrence.

{SUCCESSION PLANTING} staggering plantings at timed intervals to provide continual harvests through the season.

{TYPES} different classifications of plants.

{VARIETIES} individual colors within the same type classification.

ACKNOWLEDGMENTS

TO SCOTT: My love, thank you for believing in me and being my biggest cheerleader as I poured my heart into these pages. This book would never have been possible without your love, encouragement, and support. Thank you for being my partner in life and in love and making all of my dreams come true.

TO MY BOYS, MASON, MAVERICK, AND FINN: Being your mom is the greatest gift I've ever known. Thank you for all your love, patience, and handmade notes rooting me on.

TO MY PARENTS: Thank you for instilling in me the value of hard work, for believing in me, and for teaching me to not be afraid to push myself out of my comfort zone. Without those life lessons this book wouldn't have been possible.

TO MAMAWO AND POPO: I miss you more than you will ever know. I know you're here with me in spirit and that these pages would make you so proud.

TO CHRISTINE CHITNIS: Thank you for being there with me every step of the way and making this dream of mine a reality. Not only did your stunning photography bring my book to life, but your mentorship, friendship, hard work, support, and love have also meant the world to me. It was a dream working with you, and I am forever grateful.

TO MY INCREDIBLE AGENT SALLY EKUS AND THE EKUS GROUP: Thank you for all your hard work and for believing in me and this book. Having your support and the incredible team in my corner to navigate this new literary world has been a dream come true.

TO MY CHRONICLE TEAM, A.K.A. "TEAM SWEET PEA": I can never thank you enough. Your excitement, talent, artistry, and aesthetic made my book even more beautiful than I could've ever imagined. Thank you for believing in me, for believing in sweet peas, and for bringing *Sweet Pea School* to fruition.

TO ROGER PARSONS, DR. KEITH HAMMETT, AND PHIL JOHNSON: I am truly so inspired by each of you and your tireless dedication to these incredible flowers. Thank you so much for all of the hard work you've done over the years to bring so much beauty and joy to so many of us.

TO NICOLE: Flower friends are the best friends. Thank you for your friendship and for cheering me on as this little idea turned into something bigger than I could've ever imagined.

TO AMY: Thank you for your friendship and support throughout this process. I couldn't have done it without you.

TO FRAN: Thank you so much for your help with breeder identification. I am so appreciative!

TO FARRAH: Thank you for all your tireless work with the photo shoot and for bouncing the light just where it needed to be.

TO EVA AND KELLY: Thank you for your beautiful captures.

FINALLY, TO ALL OF MY SWEET PEA SCHOOL WORKSHOP STUDENTS: Thank you for planting the seed for me to write a book. It is because of you that I pushed myself out of my comfort zone and took this giant leap of faith. Your encouragement, excitement, and love for sweet peas has completely changed my life more than you will ever know.

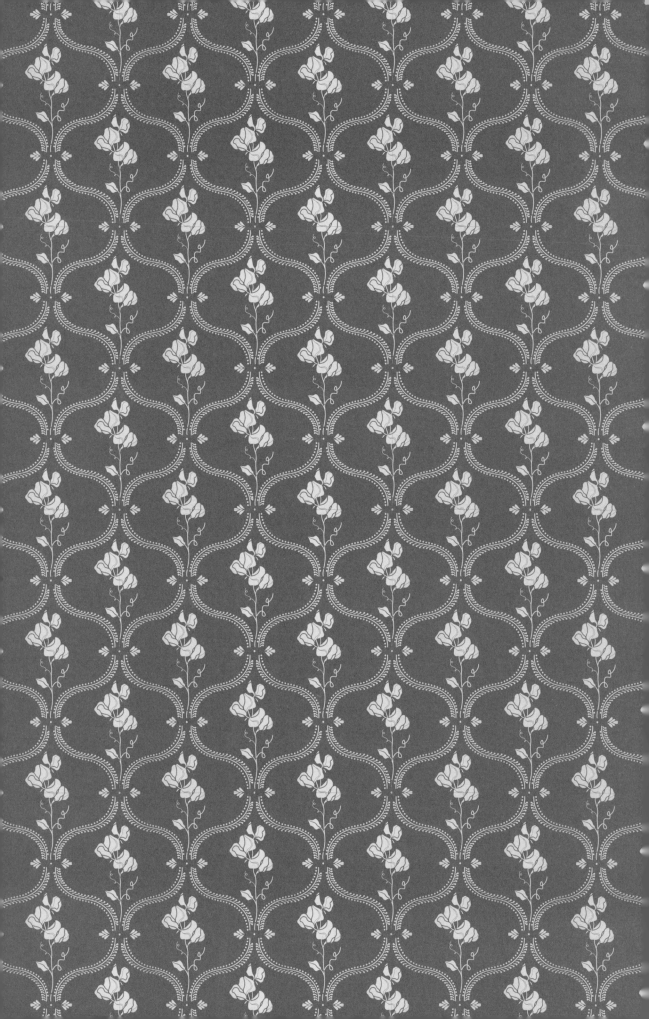